THE NEW TESTAMENT as Personal Reading

Edited by
RONAN DRURY

Templegate Publishers/Springfield, Illinois

Published in the United States
by Templegate Publishers
302 East Adams Street
P.O. Box 5152
Springfield, Illinois 62705

Copyright © Ronan Drury, 1983

All rights reserved, including the right of reproduction in whole or in part in any form.

ISBN 0-87243-122-3

CONTENTS

Introduction
   Ronan Drury vi

Performing the Scriptures . . .
   Interpretation through Living - *Nicholas Lash* 7

There Was a Birth Certainly . . .
   The Infancy Narratives - *Donal Flanagan* 19

Discipline for a New Community . . .
   The Gospel According to St. Matthew - *Donald Nicholl* ... 28

Waiting on God . . .
   The Pharisee and the Publican - *Vincent McNamara* 42

At Cross Purposes . . .
   Jesus and the Disciples in Mark - *Sean Freyne* 54

The Olive Tree in the Forum . . .
   The Letter to the Romans - *Sean Quinlan* 69

For Yours is the Kingdom . . .
   The Beatitudes - *Thomas Waldron* 85

Great Deeds in Young Churches . . .
   The Acts of the Apostles - *Donal Dorr* 99

Set Free for Freedom . . .
   The Letter to the Galatians - *Enda McDonagh* 107

The Passion According to Mark . . .
   Divine Power and Suffering - *John Riches* 118

The Resurrection . . .
   - *Josephine Newman* 131

Blood-dimmed Tide? . . .
   Thoughts on the Apocalypse - *Thomas Finan* 145

Introduction

This series of articles was meant to help readers follow the New Testament in a meditative, living way as they might read any serious literature. This kind of reading, with the familiarity and personal engagement it offers, enables Christians better to understand, assimilate and live the New Testament.

The writer of each article was asked to share his or her personal, reflective and active reading with readers of *The Furrow*. The writer would bring his or her own presuppositions and questions to the text and enter into a personal relationship with its author. The result, we hope, reflects a living exchange between the contemporary writer and the author of the New Testament text.

In the past the endeavour would have been to appropriate the text. The text would have become a possession to be explained and applied in our world. But the current understanding suggests more a dialectical interchange between reader and text. The reader brings his questions and presuppositions to challenge the text only to have them challenged in turn by the text itself.

There are many elements: allowing the light of imagination to play on the Book as book; the praying of the gospel; the Bible as art . . . It is the other side of much of the writing done about the Bible, the far side. If the near side is exegesis, this is the exegesis of the heart. It begins at the point at which the writer lays aside the commentaries and says, 'This is what the text is saying to me'.

This is by no means to devalue the more scholarly work of the professional exegete or the critical analysis of contemporary society but it is to ask people who move with some grace in their own world and in the world of the New Testament to sharpen our questions, expose our presuppositions and give shape to the Pauline hope that haunts our world.

Maynooth, June 1983

Ronan Drury
Editor, *The Furrow*

Performing the Scriptures
Interpretation through Living

Nicholas Lash

Open a copy of the New Testament, leaf through its pages. What do we see? A letter from Paul to his friends in Corinth? Matthew's account of the passion of Jesus? John's reflections on the significance of this one man whose words and work and fate, whose particular flesh, 'speak' from beyond all time and circumstance? No, we don't see anything of the kind. All that we *see* is a set of black marks on white paper.

What does one do with a set of black marks on white paper? One could decide that they make so pleasing a pattern that their best use would be to frame them and hang them on the wall. (That is not a completely far-fetched suggestion: a friend of mine, an expert in Hebrew calligraphy, once wrote a letter in Hebrew to my wife; it hangs in the hall, not for its message, but for its appearance. Family Bibles are sometimes like that, decorative rather than functional.) But, confronted with a pattern of black marks that we recognize as a form of notation, what we usually do is to try to make sense of it, to read it, to interpret it.

How does one 'read' or interpret a text? The activity is so familiar that the question may seem foolish. And yet a moment's reflection suggests that, for different kinds of text, different kinds of activity count as what we might call the primary or fundamental form of their interpretation.

Two random examples. A group of people tramping

Nicholas Lash is Norris-Hulse Professor of Theology at the University of Cambridge.

The New Testament As Personal Reading

across the hills, bits of paper in one hand, compasses in the other. What are they doing? They are engaged in what the army calls a 'map-reading exercise'. Another group, in a pub, one speaking, the others listening, are taking part in a poetry reading. (Notice that all of them, not just the speaker, are 'taking part' in the reading.)

There are some texts the interpretation of which seems to be a matter of, first, 'digging' the meaning out of the text and then, subsequently, putting the meaning to use, applying it in practice. That might be a plausible description of what someone was doing who, armed with a circuit diagram, tried to mend his television set. But it would be a most misleading description of what a judge is doing when, in the particular case before him, he interprets the law. In this case, interpretation is a creative act that could not have been predicted by a computer because it is the judge's business to 'make' the law by his interpretation of precedent. What the law means is decided by his application of it.

What it means to read or interpret a text depends in part, then, on the kind of text that is being used. Different kinds of text call for different kinds of reading. And the reader must take responsibility for the reading, for deciding what kind of text it is with which he or she is dealing. This does not mean that it is simply 'up to me' arbitrarily to decide what to do with a text. (It would be silly to sing railway timetables, rather than use them to catch trains.) What it does mean is that it is the *reading* of the text, rather than merely the text itself, the material object, the black marks on white paper, which embodies decisions as to what kinds of reading are appropriate. And the richer the text, the more complex its relationship to the culture

Performing the Scriptures

which reads and remembers it, the more varied the range of more or less appropriate readings which it evokes.

Thus (briefly to anticipate the discussion of the New Testament which I shall get round to eventually) it is possible, at least in some versions, to read the Scriptures for the beauty of their language; it is possible to read them because they speak to our condition; it is possible to read them because they speak of Jesus; it is possible to read them because they speak the mystery of God. And however we decide to take them, the decision to take them one way rather than another is *ours*, at each reading. We cannot pass the buck. It is therefore incumbent upon us to read as competently and responsibly as we can.

This raises another set of problems, because not just anybody can read just any text. I am useless at reading circuit diagrams, and I can't read Polish. Confronted by such texts, I have to pass the buck to the appropriate expert.

Open a copy of the New Testament, leaf through its pages. If it happens to be a copy of the Greek text, most of us would be stuck from the start. We would need the help of the expert. But do we also need his help in the case of texts that were written in, or have been translated into, a language with which we are familiar? And, if the answer is 'Yes', what is the relationship between the expert's contribution to the task of interpretation, and that of the 'general reader'?

At the time of the Reformation, the attempt was made to rescue the New Testament from the clutches of the ecclesiastical authorities, who claimed that they alone were competent to interpret the text, and to place it once again in the hands of those for whom it was written. But a lot has happened since the inven-

The New Testament As Personal Reading

tion of the printing-press helped to bring about that particular revolution in the reading of the New Testament. We have become very conscious of the fact that there is no such thing as what any text 'obviously' means. What a text obviously *seems* to mean, at first sight, may turn out, on examination, to have little or nothing to do with what it meant to those who produced it or to those for whom it was originally produced (what did *they* make of the story of Christmas, or the Sermon on the Mount, or the trial before Pilate? And how do we know, without trying to find out?). This is by no means only true of ancient texts, produced in cultural contexts whose patterns of thought and argument, illustration and imagery, memory and expectation, were very different from our own. But it undoubtedly *is* true of such texts. And so, between the New Testament and the ordinary Christian, who seeks so to read these texts as to hear in them the Word of Life, there seem to be set up thickets of expertise, insurmountable barriers of scholarship. And, as everybody knows, there is not a line in the New Testament concerning the interpretation of which the experts are not deeply divided. If the New Testament once needed rescuing from the ecclesiastical authorities (some of whom have still perhaps too tight a grip on it) does it now need rescuing from the professors of theology?

So far, I have only tried to make four simple points. In the first place, 'reading' is always a matter of interpreting a text, of putting it to appropriate use. In the second place, what counts as an appropriate strategy of use or interpretation will depend upon the kind of text with which we are dealing. In the third place, the reader cannot avoid taking personal responsibility for the interpretative strategy which he or she employs.

Performing the Scriptures

In the fourth place, there are difficulties concerning the relationship between our use of the New Testament, as ordinary Christians, and the responsibilities of 'authoritative' interpreters, whether ecclesiastical authorities or academic experts.

I suggested earlier that, for different kinds of text, different kinds of activity count as the fundamental form of their interpretation. I would now like to illustrate this suggestion and to indicate, at the same time, something of the relationships that exist between such fundamental interpretative activity and the interpretative tasks of the scholar and critic.

There is a set of black marks on white paper which are recognizable as the score of one of Beethoven's late string quartets. Consider four people playing the quartet. What are they doing? They are interpreting the text. Even if the performance is technically faultless (and is, in that sense, a 'correct' interpretation) we might judge it to be lifeless, unimaginative. There is a creativity in interpretation which, far from being arbitrary (the players cannot do whatever they like with the score) is connected in some way with the fidelity, the 'truthfulness' of their performance.

There is, undoubtedly, an expertise which the musicians need. Behind any great performance lie years of disciplined experience. But the particular expertise necessary for good performance is neither the same as, nor in competition with, the academic skills of the textual critics who make the score available through scholarly research and the critics and musicologists who have their own contribution to make to the continuing history of Beethoven interpretation. The fundamental form of the interpretation of Beethoven consists in the performance of his texts. The academics have an indispensable but subordinate part to play in contributing to the quality and appreciation of the performance.

Since the differences between a Beethoven score and the text of the Gospel according to Matthew are more obvious than the similarities, consider another example: a company of actors and an audience performing *King Lear*. Once again, the activity upon which they are engaged is that of interpreting a text. And, once again, the quality of the interpretation depends partly upon an element of creativity that is essential to the interpretative task. We look to the actors and the producer to enable us in some measure freshly to experience and understand the play.

But, at the end of an outstanding performance of *King Lear*, is it only the *play* that we feel ourselves newly to have understood? If we say, after the performance, 'I'd never *seen* that before', are we referring only to something which we had never previously seen in the text? Or are we also referring to an element of self-discovery which the performance had helped us to achieve? And what is the relationship between these two discoveries? Might it be that, in the performance of a great work of art, a 'classic', self-discovery and the discovery of fresh meaning in the text converge? Might it be that the 'greatness' of a text lies in its inexhaustible capacity to express, to dramatize, fundamental features of the human drama?

Leaving such questions on one side for the time being, *King Lear* does seem to be another example of a text the fundamental form of the interpretation of which consists in its performance. As in the case of the musical analogy, the expertise required by actors and producer in order to perform well is of a different order from that required of the indispensable but subordinate academic interpreters: the textual critics,

Performing the Scriptures

historians of Elizabethan drama, literary critics and philosophers.

What both these examples suggest is that there are at least some texts that only begin to deliver their meaning in so far as they are 'brought into play' through interpretative performance. This is also true, I suggest, of such other 'works of art' as the poem, the novel and the story.

Now, at last, we are getting to the point. Not all the texts of the New Testament are stories but, taken together, they 'tell the story' of Jesus and the first Christian communities. I want to suggest, firstly, that, although the texts of the New Testament may be read, and read with profit, by anyone interested in Western culture and concerned for the human predicament, the fundamental form of the *Christian* interpretation of Scripture is the life, activity and organisation of the believing community. Secondly, that Christian practice, as interpretative action, consists in the *performance* of texts which are construed as 'rendering', bearing witness to, one whose words and deeds, discourse and suffering, 'rendered' the truth of God in human history. The performance of the New Testament enacts the conviction that these texts are most appropriately read as the story of Jesus, the story of everyone else, and the story of God.

In comparison with some other 'models' of the relationship between interpretation and discipleship, Bible and theology, Scripture and tradition, this suggestion does at least have the merit of reminding us that the *poles* of Christian interpretation are not, in the last analysis, written texts (the text of the New Testament on the one hand and, on the other, whatever appears today in manuals of theology and catechetics, papal encyclicals, pastoral letters, etc.) but patterns of human action: what was said and done and suffered, then, by Jesus and his disciples, and what is said and done and suffered, now, by those who seek to share his obedience and his hope. We talk of 'Holy' Scripture, and for good reason. And yet it is not, in fact, the *script* that is 'holy', but the people: the company who perform the script.

Moreover, as my musical and dramatic analogies were intended to indicate, the model has the further advantage of keeping the experts firmly in their place while acknowledging their skills to be indispensable. To say that the fundamental form of the Christian interpretation of Scripture is the performance of the biblical text affords no licence to that 'fundamentalism' which is still a depressingly widespread feature of popular preaching and catechesis. In order to do the job properly, Christian discipleship, the performative interpretation of Scripture, needs (just as much as does the interpretation of Beethoven and Shakespeare) the services of scholarship and critical reflection.

I have been at pains to emphasize that those who engage in the activity of reading a text bear personal responsibility for their reading. But to say that the responsibility is personal is not to say that it is executed by isolated individuals. Personal responsibility is not the same thing as 'private judgment'. Christian living, construed as the interpretative performance of Scripture is, for two reasons, necessarily a collaborative enterprise.

This is so, firstly, because (as I have pointed out already) the performers need the help of the 'experts'. The second reason arises from the nature of the texts: it takes two to tango and rather more to perform *King Lear*.

Performing the Scriptures

For even the most dedicated musician or actor, the interpretation of Beethoven or Shakespeare is a part-time activity. Off-stage, the performers relax, go shopping, dig the garden. But there are some texts the fundamental form of the interpretation of which is a full-time affair because it consists in their enactment as the social existence of an entire human community. The Scriptures, I suggest, are such texts. This is what is meant by saying that the fundamental form of the Christian interpretation of Scripture is the life, activity and organisation of the believing community. The performance of Scripture *is* the life of the Church. It is no more possible for an isolated individual to perform *these* texts than it is for him to perform a Beethoven quartet or a Shakespearean tragedy.

Another analogy may help. The fundamental form of the political interpretation of the American Constitution is the life, activity and organisation of American society. That society exists (not without change, conflict and confusion) as the *enactment* of its Constitution. Similarly, we might say that the Scriptures are the 'constitution' of the Church.

Even in the case of societies that have a written constitution, the interpretation of that constitution is an unending enterprise. Times change, circumstances change. The 'meaning' of the constitution is never definitively 'captured'; it is, ever and again, sought and constructed. Similarly, each new performance of Beethoven or Shakespeare is a new event in the history of the meaning of the text. There is no such thing as an interpretation that is 'final' and 'definitive' in the sense of bringing that history to an end.

But how can this be true of the New Testament? How can we square the recognition that the history of the meaning of the text continues indefinitely with

The New Testament As Personal Reading

the ascription of *finality* to God's work of revelation in Jesus the Christ? This is a large question; all I can do is offer a couple of clues.

In the first place, the range of appropriate interpretations of a dramatic or literary text is constrained by what the text 'originally meant'. This is what keeps the historians and textual critics in business. Good Shakespearean production, for example, presupposes an effective and abiding interest in what was originally meant. The author retains his authority if it is *his* text, and not some other, that we seek to interpret.

In the second place, in order to understand a text we have to understand the question to which it is an answer. We may give up the enterprise: there are texts that we no longer bother to read, or which we feel ourselves unable to make sense of. But so long as the enterprise continues, so long as we continue to seek to perform *these* texts, we are continuing to endorse that which we take the texts to have originally meant.

And if the question to which the text sought originally to provide an answer was a question concerning the ultimate and definitive character, outcome and significance of human history; and if the answer (expressed in the text) consisted in the ascription of ultimate, unsurpassable, effective significance to the words and work and death of one man, then, to continue appropriately to perform this text is to continue to ascribe such significance to this man.

To put it very simply: as the history of the meaning of the text continues, we can and must tell the story differently. But we do so under constraint: what we may *not* do, if it is *this* text which we are to continue to perform, is to tell a different story.

There is another objection to the model I am pro-

Performing the Scriptures

posing which needs briefly to be considered. *King Lear* is fiction; the Gospels are, in some sense, historical. They therefore carry a built-in reference to particular, completed past events which renders them resistant to the interpretative relativism to which fictional constructions are subject.

Once again, all I can do here is to offer some clues to the resolution of the dilemma. In the first place, we would not bother to continue performing *King Lear* (except as a museum piece) if we no longer believed in it, if we no longer found it 'true to life'. Some people, I think, give up the practice of Christianity for a similar reason.

In the second place, however, the New Testament texts do not simply give symbolic, narrative expression to certain fundamental and pervasive features of the human drama (although Christians are apt to overlook the extent to which the fact that they *do* do this is part of their enduring power and attractiveness). They also express their authors' confidence in one man in whom the mystery of divine action is seen to have been embodied and disclosed.

We can perform *King Lear* even if the central character in the text had no particular prototype. But if we were to read the New Testament on this supposition, or on the supposition that the accuracy of the portrait did not matter, we should have excised a central element from what the text originally meant. We would be telling a different story.

Moreover, the texts of the New Testament not only purport to express the fact and significance of one man but, in doing so, they refer both fact and significance to the mystery of divine action. It follows that, for the practice of Christianity, the performance of the biblical text, to be true, it must be not only 'true to

The New Testament As Personal Reading

life', but 'true to *his* life'; and not only 'true to his life', but 'true to God'. That it is so, and may be made so, is at once our responsibility, our hope and our prayer.

I have been suggesting that the fundamental form of the Christian interpretation of Scripture is the life, activity and organisation of the Christian community, construed as performance of the biblical text. The best illustration of what this might mean is, of course, the celebration of the Eucharist. Here, that interpretative performance in which all our life consists — all our suffering and care, compassion, celebration, struggle and obedience — is dramatically distilled, focused, concentrated, rendered explicit. In this context, the principal forms of discourse are 'practical': in praise, confession, petition, they seek to *enact* the meanings which they embody. And if, in the liturgy of the Word, the story is told, it is told not so that it may merely be relished or remembered, but that it may be *performed*, in the following of Christ.

At the end of a performance of *Lear*, the actors leave the stage, remove their costumes, 'return to life'. But, for each Christian actor, the performance of the biblical text ends only at death. The stage on which we enact our performance is that wider human history in which the Church exists as the 'sacrament', or dramatic enactment, of history's ultimate meaning and hope. If the texts of the New Testament are to express that which Christian faith declares them capable of expressing, the quality of our *humanity* will be the criterion of the adequacy of the performance. And yet this criterion is, in the last resort, hidden from us in the mystery of God whose meaning for man we are bidden to enact.

There was a Birth Certainly . . .
— the Infancy Narratives

Donal Flanagan

I was surprised to see a letter in the papers recently doubting the existence of Jesus. It was from a Rationalist (capital R) source — the Rationalist Press Association. It carried my mind back over decades to tomes of apologetics on which the dust now rests and out of that dusty past the name Drews, perhaps Arthur Drews, emerged. He had advanced the same thesis that Jesus was just a story-book figure not a real man. And we had refuted him placing a heavy emphasis on the value of our Christian records as credible historical sources. We had indeed inherited a tradition of apologetics in which any denial of the reality of Jesus, or indeed any docetic nonsense stood no chance of survival.

Docetism? Not an outright denial of his existence like Drews' and Rationalist views but an erosion of his earthiness, of his humanness. A very ancient error, a strange error to have emerged so soon after his lifetime. Rejected already with great force by Bishop Ignatius of Antioch who died just after the turn of the first century. We still have a letter which Ignatius, condemned to death, wrote to the Church at Smyrna in which he says that it is a matter of great importance to him as he goes to his death for his beliefs that the people he leaves behind should be steadfast, firmly convinced in their faith that Jesus Christ is 'truly of the race of David according to the flesh, Son of God according to the will and power of God, born of

---

Donal Flanagan is a Radio Producer with Radio Telefís Éireann.

The New Testament As Personal Reading

a virgin, baptized by John . . .' (*Smyrn 1:* PG 5, 707-708).

Ignatius fought this peculiar heresy which called in question the true flesh-and-blood manhood of Jesus, by referring to the Scriptural account of his descent from David, his recorded acts in his life on earth, his suffering and death as a man at Calvary. In his letter to the church at Tralles he writes:

> Close your ears, then, if anyone preaches to you without speaking of Jesus Christ. Christ was of David's line. He was the son of Mary. He was truly born and ate and drank. He was in truth persecuted in the days of Pontius Pilate and in truth and really crucified and gave up his spirit in the sight of all heaven and all earth and the powers of the lower world (*ad Trall.* 8).

We find the same concern with the historical reality of Jesus of Nazareth, his life and works in the somewhat later writings of Irenaeus, bishop of Lyons, who lived in the second century. He was the great opponent of Gnostic thinking which he felt would, if left unchecked, dissolve the substance of the Christian faith. Its teachings if unopposed would put the reality of Christian salvation at risk and notably cast doubt on the full earthly reality of Jesus which Irenaeus saw as the hinge on which salvation turned. Irenaeus, too, like Ignatius before him, appealed to the Scriptural record — it was all written down there, his birth, his life, his death. There was a death certainly and it was our salvation, the death of one man Jesus Christ.

But to die a man has first to be born. . . . There was a birth certainly but there was so much more in the scriptural infancy account and it was all of this

There Was a Birth Certainly . . .

together which passed into the Christian consciousness which surrounds the feast of Christmas.

O HOLY NIGHT

The resonances of the Christian feast of Christmas sound far outside the walls of churches, of convents, of monasteries where, in spare splendour the offices and liturgies of the Church are performed with joy. The feast carries over into the home, into the celebration of the family round the table, into the lighted candle in the window, into the welcoming of the stranger and wanderer to the hearth. This birth we celebrate is a birth for all. This birth is a new beginning. Because it is a new beginning all the songs we sing about it are songs of hope, fulfilment, renewal. Because it is a birth for all, the songs about it are about love between all whose brother he became.

Sadly in our society it is not permitted to men to cry or I could tell you of my tears each time I hear Luciano Pavarotti sing Adolph Adam's 'O Holy Night'. There are tears in the joy of Christmas but they are tears for mercy received and for mercy repeatedly given. The words of this song alone cannot catch the vibrancy of human feeling which is present when a great voice joins them to the music but even unadorned they are still Christmas, the feast of the Birth.

> O holy night! the stars are brightly shining,
> It is the night of the dear Saviour's birth;
> Long lay the world in sin and error pining,
> Till he appear'd, and the soul felt its worth,
> A thrill of hope and weary world rejoices,
> For yonder breaks a new and glorious morn,
> Fall on your knees, oh hear the angel voices!
> O night divine! O night when Christ was born.

The New Testament As Personal Reading

Led by the light of Faith serenely beaming
With glowing hearts by his cradle we stand;
So led by the light of a star sweetly gleaming,
Here came the wise men from the Orient land.
The King of kings lay thus in lowly manger,
In all our trials born to be our friend;
He knows our need, to our weakness no stranger;
Behold your King! before the Lowly bend!
Behold your King! Your King! Before him bend!

Truly he taught us to love one another;
His law is Love and his Gospel is Peace.
Chains shall he break, for the slave is our brother,
And in his name all oppression shall cease.
Sweet hymns of joy in grateful chorus raise,
Let all with us praise his Holy name.
Christ is the Lord, then ever, ever praise we,
His pow'r and glory ever more proclaim.

There are many other hymns and songs of Christmas which have become flesh of flesh and bone of bone for Christians. All share the simplicities of the gospel story, all set the coming of the Saviour in a thoroughly human and familiar context. This the gospel stories do and so do the later writers who added details like ox and ass. And writers, painters, sculptors, musicians, wood carvers, poets and artists of every kind have conspired over the centuries that we should have a human and familiar Christmas, that the birth of Jesus should be in a familiar context and all the details should be in place.

THE CRIB

This concreteness of Christmas, can be seen perhaps nowhere to better effect than in our cribs of Christmas. They present the birth of Jesus in the manger,

There Was a Birth Certainly . . .

surrounded by familiar figures, dressed in familiar colours, marked by familiar symbols — the shepherds carrying lambs, the Magi, gifts, and over the stable the 'star of Bethlehem', the heavenly marker for the event.

This pictorial and artistic representation founds itself directly on the words of Scripture. It only accepts marginal extra details like the ox and the ass from extra-biblical sources. It has sunk very deeply into the Christian consciousness of Christmas and has strongly reinforced the idea among Catholic believers that the infancy narratives are to be taken literally in every detail as history. The narratives are viewed as factual historical accounts of happenings before, during and after the birth of Jesus which share the historical character of the birth itself. This position, that all details mentioned in the infancy narratives are equally historical, means for those who hold it, that if the historical character of one detail is denied then the whole is at risk including the historicity of the birth itself.

This was indeed the Catholic style and approach in regard to the infancy narratives of Matthew and Luke when I was a student in the forties and fifties. The accepted theology and the popular devotional understanding and representation of the events of these chapters were in agreement. This, indeed, had been the theological style for a very long time. Many Christian authors had spent many laborious hours on the nature of the star, the place of the sojourn in Egypt, its exact duration, on the habits of Galilean shepherds, in order to build out the details of Jesus' first years amongst us.

The New Testament As Personal Reading

THE QUESTIONING

This basic insistence on the historicity of all details in the infancy narrative came under pressure in the theological field from the end of the nineteenth century as advanced Protestant exegetical studies took a more and more relaxed view of the importance of the infancy materials and a more liberal view of the historical character of the material. To counter this trend Catholic Church authority (in this case, the Pontifical Biblical Commission) issued in the opening decades of this century, a series of decrees in which the historicity of various questioned parts of Scripture was insisted upon as a view mandatory on Catholic scholars. These directives did not solve the problem; they rather postponed it in the manner of a dam halting a river's flow. The decrees are understandable in that they were issued at the time of the modernist crisis but they had the result of blocking debate on these questions and specifically on the infancy narratives, for the best part of fifty years in the Catholic Church.

It was only with Pope Pius XII's encouragement of Catholic biblical scholarship in the nineteen forties and fifties that these concealed questions came into the open and a scholarly debate among Catholic authors could begin. Thus the infancy narratives figured in debate in the period before and during Vatican II and a new approach to the question of the nature of these narratives began gradually to emerge. This was a particularly difficult area for scholars because their findings, where they presented a new approach to the materials, often tended to frighten people accustomed to the older presumption that every detail of the infancy accounts was to be taken as fact. In addition, in the sphere of catechetics, the transpo-

There Was a Birth Certainly . . .

sition of the findings of exegetes and biblical theologians to the popular level wasn't an easy task and, indeed, it was sometimes incompetently done, with the result that people were left with an insufficient grasp of the new and a sense of the old collapsing about them.

THE ACCOUNTS

John and Mark in their gospels give no account of the birth of Jesus from Mary. Matthew and Luke do — but their two accounts are not the same. Older commentators resorted to harmonisation as a method of dealing with differences in these accounts as they tried to produce a consecutive narrative taking details from both evangelists. The crib, indeed, presents a very interesting practical case of harmonisation at the popular level containing as it often does, St Luke's shepherds, St Matthew's magi and the ox and the ass who are mentioned by neither evangelist.

Modern scholars by contrast tend to look at differences in the two accounts — and there are differences — and to try to discover the reason for these. When we look at the Matthaean and Lucan accounts which are popularly called the infancy narratives we find that they are contrary to one another in a number of details. For example:

Cf. Lk. 2:22, 39 with Mt. 2:16:

Luke: the family returned peaceably to Nazareth after the birth at Bethlehem.
Matthew: the child was almost two years old when the family fled from Bethlehem to Egypt.

The New Testament As Personal Reading

These differences suggest that it may not be correct to approach each account, even where it appears to be giving historical details, as simple unvarnished factual history. Further there is the fact that in each of the two accounts there is a heavy drawing on the Old Testament Scriptures which suggests strongly that for these evangelists the infancy narratives formed a bridge from the Old Testament to the gospel. They are, therefore, something apart, something outside that main body of that gospel material which has a claim to be anchored in the reminiscences of those who were with Jesus from after his baptism to his death. The infancy narratives are to be understood, then, as the final stage of the putting together of our present canonical gospels, a different kind of material which needs to be understood in the light of the emergent christology of the Infant Church. Shaped by each evangelist to the needs and concerns of his gospel, they are in a very strong sense vehicles of the theology of the evangelist.

When all this has been said, however, we must return to the fact that the two narratives in spite of being independently produced share points which are clearly affirmed in each account and the majority of these points focus on the birth itself. This agreement between the two accounts would suggest a common infancy tradition older than the accounts in Matthew and Luke.

Among these points are:

(1) The conception of the child of Mary is not through intercourse with her husband (Mt. 1, 20, 23, 25 and Lk. 1, 34).
(2) The birth takes place at Bethlehem (Mt. 2, 1 and Lk. 2, 4-6).

There Was a Birth Certainly . . .

(3) The birth is chronologically related to the reign of Herod the Great (Mt. 2, 1 and Lk. 1, 5).
(4) The child is reared at Nazareth (Mt. 2, 23, and Luke 2, 39).

What we have then in the infancy narratives are accounts of the birth of Jesus presented in a highly developed theological form which the evangelists saw as suitable introductions to the career and significance of Jesus. These accounts form part of these gospels because they present the *Good News* of *the birth* of Jesus the Son of God acting for the salvation of mankind.

The birth of Jesus is presented in the New Testament in a strongly Jewish context — Davidic sonship, promise, prophecy, Messiahship. It is broadened by Matthew with the Wise Men from the East so that the Epiphany in the Christian calendar becomes the feast of the revelation of Christ to the Gentiles. But Christmas itself, the feast at the turn of the year, replaces the old pagan nature festival of the rebirth of the sun with a new historical birth of the Saviour of the World, Jesus of Nazareth, the *Sol Invictus*. There was a birth certainly. . . .[1]

---

1. See Raymond Brown: *The Birth of the Messiah* (Doubleday. Image. Garden City, New York, 1979) — a classical presentation of the problems of the infancy narratives for the popular reader and for the scholar. I found it very helpful in preparing this article.

Discipline for a New Community
— the Gospel according to St Matthew

Donald Nicholl

At first sight it might seem a fruitless undertaking to search in the Gospel of St Matthew for a discipline for a new community. After all we have evidence that untold commentators have been commenting on this Gospel since the days of St Ignatius of Antioch (+ 115) and Papias, bishop of Hierapolis (+ 130). And even before that they must have been doing so. So what can a disciple learn from it that is new?

Almost as though he had anticipated the question, St Matthew records a saying of Jesus which answers the question, a saying, moreover, that may well describe the calling of Matthew himself. He tells us that Jesus said, 'Every scribe who becomes a disciple of the kingdom of heaven is like a householder who brings out from his store-room things both new and old' (13:52).

By those words Jesus not only accurately pinpoints the task of the good scribe but he also puts his finger upon the scribe's experience. By this I mean that all of us who study the holy scriptures have the uncanny experience, at one time or another, of reading a scriptural text which we have previously read or heard hundreds of times, perhaps even thousands of times, but which suddenly seems to leap out of the page and strike us with its meaning in such a way that we say to ourselves, 'Well, I have read that passage hundreds of times before and studied it and meditated upon it, but until now I never realized what it meant!'

Donald Nicholl is Rector of the Ecumenical Institute for Advanced Theological Studies at Tantur, Jerusalem.

Discipline for a New Community

And although most of us have had such an experience many times we still continue to be astonished all over again every time it happens to us. Which in one way is not surprising because insights that are new are, quite simply, new. They are not something we could have worked out for ourselves or something we could have anticipated from past experience. They are moments when God illumines our mind to some truth which we could never have hit upon for ourselves in a million years. For some reason we find this difficult to accept — that there is genuine newness in the universe and that all genuine newness issues fresh from the hand of God. Any seeming newness that does not, in fact, come from God is reducible in the end to merely a new form of old sin. For the same reason we cannot *plan* a new community because what we *plan* will only be a different form of the old community. Only a new creation of God can liberate us from servitude to old sin, of whatever form. For 'what we are to be in the future has not yet been revealed', as St John says 'All we know is that when it is revealed we shall be like him because we shall see him as he really is' (1 John 3:2). Or, as St Paul says, 'for anyone who is in Christ there is a new creation' (2 Cor. 5:17), not just the old one rigged up differently.

Recently I heard a famous theologian giving an account of how it had happened to him to see things anew. He said that for almost fifty years he had been reading the Scriptures and then one day the Bible became for him something completely new. He spoke of how it was as though he had been living in a darkened room all his life until on that day someone switched on the electric light and he was able to see everything in the room where previously he had only fumbled around. The reason he gave for this sudden

The New Testament As Personal Reading

illumination was that he had lately spent some time in Latin America amongst the poor, the marginalized, the oppressed, and as a result had begun to read the Bible from their point of view, the standpoint from which it was meant to be read.

I did not press him to analyse why, in his previous fifty years, he had been approaching the Bible blindly — in fact I had a fairly good idea of why that was because his previous pronouncements on Scripture had often reminded me of the judgement made by Langmead Casserly upon a certain way of reading the Scriptures: 'That is a strange way of reading the Word of God from which no Word of God emerges'. And how very many of us who are professionals in this field fall under that judgement! I sometimes compare us to water diviners who go around with our professional divining rods, tapping on the surface of the earth saying, '*Here* there may be a spring' or '*There* will be a spring', but we ourselves never dig deep down below the surface in order to taste of the springs. Which is why it could not be said in relation to us, 'anyone who drinks the water that I shall give will never be thirsty again; the water that I shall give will turn into a spring inside him, welling up to eternal life' (John 4:13-14). Instead we are more like those Pharisees to whom Jesus said, 'Alas for you, Scribes and Pharisees, you hypocrites! You who shut up the kingdom of heaven in men's faces, neither going in yourselves nor allowing others to go in who want to' (Matt. 23:13). There is here some deep mystery, which no human being can fathom, expressed in Jesus' words, 'I bless you, Father, Lord of heaven and of earth, for hiding these things from the learned and the clever and revealing them to mere children. Yes, Father, for that is what it pleased you to do' (Matt.

Discipline for a New Community

11:25). The mere children are those who know the location of perhaps only one spring. But they dig deep until they get to that spring and never thirst again.

Not, of course, that learning itself necessarily blocks up the spring of eternal life or shuts up the kingdom of heaven. It is obviously helpful, for instance, to know that the Greek *to hagion* in Matthew 7:6 may be a mistranslation of an Aramaic word meaning a 'ring', i.e. of gold, which affords a parallel with the pearls not to be cast before swine. But such knowledge can only too easily retain our attention on the surface of the Scriptures and so prevent us from finding the deep springs of eternal life.

But how are we to avoid that blockage? I have already told of how one famous theologian did so, by living with the oppressed in Latin America. But that is not a possibility for all of us, so perhaps it will be helpful if I indicate how it happened, though less dramatically, that the Scriptures became electric for me so that whenever I have since read them truly a Word of God has emerged for me. It is especially appropriate that I should do so here since it came about by way of St Matthew's Gospel.

And it happened in this way.

In those days I worked in a university where everyone seemed to be scurrying around with bits of memoranda for one another; or else they would be perpetually telephoning one another. Partly in order to slow both them and myself down I let it be known that I would not be available for anyone, the vice-chancellor included — indeed him especially — between the hours of nine and ten in the morning. Because I would be studying. I did not feel it necessary to say that I would be studying Scripture, because there are limits to what people can take. But that, in fact, is

The New Testament As Personal Reading

what I did.

I would very slowly read a few verses of St Matthew's Gospel both aloud and silently, both in the Greek and in English. Everything about the text that puzzled me I would try to clarify but the only things I wrote down, on a piece of scrap paper, were the words that in the Quaker phrase 'spoke to my condition'. My 'condition', my special needs, what the Lord was telling me to do, in what ways my life needed to change, all such themes became clearer in my heart and mind as the days and weeks went by. Until it gradually came about that every time I touched the Word of God I could taste the spring inside me welling up to eternal life. Not that the same theme emerges for everyone who studies in that way, nor does the same person always find himself led into the same theme every time; at one time our condition requires one word and at another time another. But always it is the same Word, the Word of life, inexhaustibly rich.

What happens, then, when we go to St Matthew's Gospel in this fashion, slowly reading in order to discover what the Lord is telling us there about a discipline for a new community?

It is at least comforting to recognize from the very first that St Matthew's Gospel, more than any of the others, arose out of the needs of a community and was therefore addressed to the needs of a community. We can be sure of this not just because Matthew is the only Gospel that uses the Greek word *ekklesia*, the equivalent of the Hebrew *qahal*, meaning the elect community of God; nor that Matthew is the only Gospel in which we are told of Jesus' words to Peter, 'Thou art Peter, and upon this rock (*Petra*) I will build my church' (16:17). It is much more that every part of the Gospel is permeated by the sense of community,

Discipline for a New Community

full of directions for holding the community together. Because Matthew's community is a community under threat, not only from external persecution — though that threat looms like a dark cloud over the Gospel (5:10, 11, 12, 44; 10:23; 23:24) — but equally through the danger of betrayal from within, since not everyone who cries 'Lord, Lord' can be counted on as a faithful member of the community (7:15-23).

Matthew's community, moreover, is preoccupied, as we in the late twentieth century are preoccupied, with the sense that the world is soon to come to an end, though we do not know exactly when. The Gospel expresses this sense particularly in chapters 24 and 25 which are so concerned with signs for the end of the world. How double-edged such signs may be was brought home to me a year or two ago when I was arranging for E. F. Schumacher, author of *Small is Beautiful*, to come to my university in California as visiting professor. Over the telephone Schumacher said to me that he was unable to come the following year owing to previous engagements. 'That's all right', I said, 'you can come the year after — I don't expect that the world will have come to an end by that time!' There was a slight pause before Schumacher answered slowly and deliberately, in a foreboding voice, 'I wouldn't be so sure of that.'

Three months later Schumacher was dead. And when I heard the news of his death I remembered that last sentence of his and thought 'Yes, the world did come to an end for him before the next year.' And for all of us Schumacher's words represent a salutary gloss upon the 24th and 25th chapters of Matthew's Gospel, sharpening our awareness that all human beings and their communities must live with a sense that their end is coming, even though they do not

The New Testament As Personal Reading

know when. The Roman Empire came to an end and so did the British; so will the American and the Soviet Empires; so will the religious orders and *communidades de base* on which so much stress is nowadays laid; and so will any new community which we ourselves may help to found. Yet no matter how long or how short the existence of the new community may be, the period of its existence will be fruitful and give rise to yet other new communities, (just as Schumacher's short span was so fruitful) so long as the new community, like Schumacher, is constantly aware that the end is near and that at any moment the Lord may dissolve us. Either we dissolve, or, like many present day secular and religious communities that we all know of, we become petrified and sterile. Yet in order for a community to hold together, even for a limited span, there must obviously be a whole series of directions for its members, establishing a discipline for them. As we have said previously, Matthew's Gospel is full of such directions. And once the Word of God has become electric, powerful, for any of us, we have to take those directions with total seriousness.

We hear, for instance, that at the judgement Our Lord will tell us whether we fed him when he was hungry or gave him a drink when he was thirsty, took him in when he was a stranger, clothed him when he was naked and visited when he was sick or in prison. Does that mean we have literally to do every one of those things? No, said a priest friend of mine who one day discovered that I had verses 31-46 of Matthew 25 inscribed in large letters on a placard on the wall of my room, meant to serve as an examination of conscience in which I used to say, 'When did I last feed anyone who was hungry? When did I last take in a stranger?', and so on down the list. My priest friend upbraided me rather sharply and said that my practice was just another form of the very legalism which Jesus had come to eliminate. At first I was somewhat abashed by my friend's reprimand, and even took down my wall placard. But on subsequent reflection, especially when I saw how far astray my priest friend's opposition to 'legalism' led him, I realized that his reaction did not do justice to the delicate balance of Matthew's Gospel. Certainly his Gospel contains some most dramatic warnings against legalism, as for instance when he defends his disciples against the Pharisees for having picked and eaten ears of corn on the Sabbath: 'Have you not read what David did when he and his followers were hungry — how he went into the house of God and how he ate the loaves of offering which neither he nor his followers were allowed to eat, but which were for the priests alone? . . . the Son of Man is master of the Sabbath.'

Nevertheless Jesus came not to abolish the Law, or the Prophets, but to complete them. And whilst it is true that one should not get stuck in the particular formulations of law (which is legalism), at the same time we have to carry them out faithfully for long periods as a way of fulfilling that Law (Torah) which cannot be formulated — precisely because it is inexhaustible. Moreover the list which we find in Matthew 25 is not situated in the realm of formulations but points rather into the sphere of the Law, that inexhaustible matrix out of which all particular formulations emerge.

So I put my placard back on the wall again. And though I do not try to tick off every one of Jesus' demands in the hope that I shall be justified when I have ticked them all off, still I do consider that I have good

The New Testament As Personal Reading

grounds for making a searching self-examination if I discover that in recent months I have not fulfilled *any* of the particular demands on that list.

For there is no evading the truth that to be a disciple of Jesus is the most demanding call that any human being can receive, and Matthew's Gospel is especially harsh in the language that it uses to drive home the total nature of those demands. One after another the images and sayings strike raw upon one's nerves as one reads his Gospel: am I such a one as calls his brother a 'renegade'? Hell fire for me, if I am. Do I lust after a woman in my heart? Then I am an adulterer. Have I spoken a calumnious word? Then I shall answer for it on the day of judgement. One after another the indelible phrases come crashing through one's egotistic defences until one begins to ask whether one may not after all be the salt that has lost its savour and is now good for nothing but to be cast out and trampled underfoot.

Is there an explanation as to why Matthew should pile up absolute demands in such a fashion?

I believe there is; and it is very simple. I believe that Matthew had seen and experienced what happens to those of us who are called by Jesus but who fall away from our calling. When he uses that favourite phrase of his that 'there will be weeping and gnashing of teeth', Matthew is not conjuring up fantasies; he is recording something that he has himself seen happening, a falling away so terrible that no physical loss or suffering can be compared to it. Precisely such weeping and wailing, though in a more subdued mode, has been hauntingly recorded in our own day by a journalist who became the confidant of Franz Stangl, the Austrian Catholic who served as the commandant of the death camp at Treblinka. Not long before he died,

Discipline for a New Community

in prison, in 1972, Stangl described how in 1938 he was a country policeman in Austria when the German troops marched in. He and the one other policeman at their country station feared that they would lose their jobs when the Nazis took over so they decided to pretend to the new regime that they had each been secret Nazis for some years; they agreed to back each other up in that 'white lie'. In such a way they would keep their jobs. From that moment onwards Stangl was swept upward, higher and higher within the Nazi party, until eventually he reached the pinnacle of Treblinka where he was responsible for the deaths of thousands of Jews.

Looking back upon that episode from his prison cell when he was on the verge of dying, Stangl slowly, hauntingly, said, 'As I looked ahead in 1938, the forty or so years of life before me seemed so sweet.' And then, after a long pause, he murmured, 'If only I could have died then'.

What would Stangl not have given, on the verge of death, to be able to wipe out those years since 1938? Would he not have said *Amen* to those words in Matthew's Gospel, 'If your hand or your foot should cause you to sin, cut it off and throw it away: it is better for you to enter into life crippled or lame than to have two hands or two feet and be thrown into eternal fire. And if your eye should cause you to sin, tear it out and throw it away; it is better for you to enter into life with one eye than to have two eyes and be thrown into the hell of fire' (Matt. 18:8-9 and 5:29-30). Surely Stangl would have found no difficulty in understanding why Jesus said to the rich young man, 'If you wish to be perfect, go and sell what you own and give the money to the poor and you will have treasure in heaven' (Matt. 19:20-22). Because Stangl had begun to realize

The New Testament As Personal Reading

that a man is in Hell if he gains the whole world but loses his own soul (Matt. 16:26). In the light of Stangl's experience it is not extravagant of Jesus to say, 'You must therefore be perfect just as your heavenly Father is perfect' (Matt. 6:48); it is plain common sense because the alternative is so terrible.

And Matthew is constantly making us face such dilemmas because he knows how prone we are to try to refuse them, trying to escape from reality into the 'sweet' realm of words. Which is why he is so fierce towards those models of piety, the Pharisees, and by extension the 'super-Pharisees' (as Roman Catholics were once called by a Dominican scholar). For a certain statement that Matthew makes about the Pharisees is meant to drive all disciples of Jesus, including modern Christians, into a dilemma from which the only outlet lies into reality. That statement is, 'And when Jesus completed his teaching the crowds were amazed because he taught them as one having authority and not like the Scribes and Pharisees.'

The acuteness of the dilemma that this statement presents to a disciple of Jesus never struck me, strangely enough, until the day when I was reading the passage in Russian. In that version the word corresponding to the English word 'scribes' is *knizhniki*, from the word *knig*, meaning a 'book'. In other words, the scribes were 'bookmen', people who based their teaching on words found in a book — as opposed to Jesus who had authority because *he knew* what he was talking about; he had put the teaching into practice; he had the authority which goes with experience. Hence a dilemma arises for his followers, because he tells us, 'All authority in heaven and on earth has been given to me. Go, therefore, make disciples of all the nations . . . and teach them to observe

Discipline for a New Community

all the commands which I gave you . . .' (Matt. 28:16-20).

Here is a kind of teaching, therefore, for which mere book knowledge is quite useless. Book knowledge, admittedly, is perfectly adequate for certain sorts of instruction; for example, if someone asks you at what times the boats sail from Holyhead to Dun Laoghaire it is sufficient for you to have a book containing the schedule, for the same is true of many other matters, that book knowledge is sufficient. But in spiritual matters book knowledge is completely useless. In spiritual teaching you have to speak with authority; and that you can only do if you have put your teaching into practice and are speaking from experience, even if it is only the experience of failure.

The dilemma, then, is this: as disciples of Jesus we have to teach spiritual truths; but on spiritual matters you can only teach if you do so with authority; and you only have authority if you have put the teaching into practice. Otherwise you are merely a bookman; your words are empty, without authority.

Let me illustrate how sharply this dilemma can bite into you. Some years ago I wrote a paragraph about Northern Ireland. In it I called attention to Jesus' command, as recorded in Matthew: 'if you are bringing your offering to the altar and there remember that your brother has something against you, leave your offering before the altar, go and be reconciled with your brother first, and then come back and present your offering' (Matt. 5:23-24). Up till that time I had always misread Jesus' command as though he was saying, 'if you have anything against your brother', whereas the command is, in fact, much more demanding since it applies if you happen to know that your brother has anything against you.

The New Testament As Personal Reading

It was clear to me then, as it is to me now, that in Northern Ireland all the Christians are aware that their brother has something against them. So I suggested that they should leave their gifts at the altar. In other words, the Mass, the Eucharist, should not be celebrated in Northern Ireland until such time as the Christians have gone to their brothers and been reconciled — given one another the kiss of peace. If there is no peace amongst brothers then they cannot approach the altar in good faith.

I had hoped that someone, preferably an archbishop or a moderator, might have taken up my suggestion; but no one whatsoever, much less an archbishop or a moderator, made any comment on it at all. Nobody was 'amazed at my teaching'! Was that because I was a bookman, speaking without authority? Or was it because my readers were Scribes and Pharisees, with eyes to see but not seeing?

In the latter case there was not much I could do about it; but in the former case the remedy was to make sure that in future I spoke with authority, that is, out of experience. I was driven, therefore, every time I approached the altar, to ask myself whether any brother or sister had anything against me; and, if so, then I must go directly to them and be reconciled. To do so can be an excruciating experience, especially if the grievance has grown green with age; there is the fear of being misunderstood, mocked, rejected and told to go to Hell. But also, of course, it is unfailingly liberating.

However, I still remain conscious that in spite of my visits to brothers and sisters who have something against me, I may even now be speaking as a bookman because I have failed to face up to my own failures and to transform them into my own experience.

Discipline for a New Community

So I may even now be speaking without authority.

But what I *can* say with authority is that St Matthew's Gospel never lets us escape for one minute out of reality into pious words. Inexorably Matthew drives us to examine ourselves unsparingly and to put into practice every jot and tittle of Jesus' teaching. Nothing less than perfection is what is demanded of us — not in words, as if the Gospel were a blueprint for Utopia, but in deeds as the realization of the only real new community.

Waiting on God
— *The Pharisee and the Publican*

Vincent McNamara

When I was young I could not understand all the talk about experience. They told me that life cannot be rushed and that some things only come with time. They said that you learn by experience and that you cannot put an old head on young shoulders. The old dog for the hard road, and a wise old owl when you were in need of counsel. Student productions of Shakespeare, a teacher told us, were all very well but students did not know enough about life to appreciate what they were about. An old musician pronounced that nobody, however technically accomplished, should attempt the later Beethoven piano sonatas until he was thirty. I suspected all of this. I could not understand how this golden wisdom could not be packaged and dispensed to us. Why didn't they simply tell us what they knew and not have us wait? It looked like some last-ditch attempt by an older generation to defend their dwindling territory against the incursions of hungry youth.

About all of this I know a bit more now and it seems to colour my faith. I know now that it takes time — life-time — to learn about being a human being. Because it does, it takes time to learn about the gospels. You have to let life teach you the questions. It sounds woefully banal to say it but it takes time — life-experience — to learn about God. There is a young person's God and a God for the middle-aged. Youth can dare,

---

Vincent McNamara is a member of St Patrick's Missionary Society. He lectures in Moral Theology at St Patrick's College, Co. Wicklow, Ireland.

Waiting on God

wants to get on with it, does not see the problems, does not count the cost. The coming of the kingdom awaits its strong arms. Praise God. But who is God for those whom you find saying softly that they haven't the energy they had, or that their memories are failing, or that they are too old to start new things? ('Why should the aged eagle dare?') The kingdom comes within them. They have to settle for acceptance — accepting themselves and being accepted by others. Being accepted by life, by reality — by God.

'By waiting and by calm you shall be saved,
In quiet and in trust your strength lies' (Is. 30:15).

It takes time to find not just the answers but the questions. One of the things that used to puzzle me at first about the writings of Karl Rahner was his emphasis on God as forgiving. (Another was his preoccupation with death. It is not what I am concerned with here but the connection will not be lost on those who follow my drift.) Take, for example, his short formula of Christian faith: 'God gives himself to man in an act of self-bestowal to be his true consummation, and that too even though it is presupposed in this that man is a sinner, so that this act of self-bestowal entails an attitude of forgiving love.' This says something about the human condition and, because it does, it says something about God. But it takes some life-experience in order to grow into it. Time teaches us that God is not just creator, not just liberator, not just a love that is *sui diffusivum*, but that his mercy is above all his works and ours. Theological statements should ring true to life. Time teaches us that Rahner's does.

I was confirmed about this earlier this year. I sat one night in a mission in Central Africa with a colleague — a student from earlier years. We had been together for a few days' reflection, some twenty of us. The World Service News was over and we were quiet. Then he said from beyond the pool of lamplight: 'You talked quite a bit up there about God as forgiving. I don't remember that you made so much of that when I was a student. Anyway, I wouldn't have understood then: I do now.' I didn't understand then, either. It takes time.

That much is by way of lead-in to the parable of the pharisee and the publican. I don't know much about theories of biblical stories or parables. I hope I am right in thinking that this one can be taken more or less at face value. But I have discovered that even then it depends greatly on where you are and what questions you have to put to the test. (Those in the hermeneutics business have more elegant ways of putting the matter.) When I was younger I presumed that the problem with the pharisee was that he was telling lies or adorning things a bit. But there is no suggestion in the text that he was. Later, accepting that the fellow was telling the truth, I was encouraged to interpret the story as a warning against boasting. Now I see that the issue is more fundamental. The problem with the pharisee was that he had the wrong God. The publican might have got his morals wrong but he had his God right. And that turns out to be more important. He went down to his house justified rather than the other.

I read somewhere — was it in von Balthasar's *Life*? — that St Thérèse said that Jesus would not have spent so much time on the pharisees if they were only one small sect in one small country at one time. We may find that way of putting it naive. She is on surer ground when she goes on to say that we are all pharisees. We are. We seek to justify ourselves before God. (Be a good boy/girl and God will love you. Be converted from your sins and turn to God and he will hear you. There go I *but* for the grace of God.) We have been brought up as Roman Catholics with a merit-God. That is why we need to think more of the story of the pharisee and the publican and allow the implications of it to speak quietly into the clamour of our lives. There is a change, I think, but it is barely perceptible. I recently asked a post-graduate student of theology ('But that was in another country . . .') what he thought about the Catholic doctrine of merit. He replied that he had never heard of it. I don't know if that says more about his training or about shifts in theology. When I gave him a rough outline of the matter he looked at me with something between disbelief and horror.

Rahner is right. We need to build forgiveness into our very idea of God. When we do, we are not busying ourselves with some fussy decoration on our Christianity. We are asking foundation-questions about the human condition. We are asking who we are and where we come from and what we may hope for. What I know now is that the parable is saying, so much more successfully than Paul did, that we are all sinners and all stand in need of the mercy of God. It is saying that all talk about striving and merit — and some of the talk about conversion and repentance — can lead us astray not only in one tract of theology but in the whole. It can distort our idea of God. We are weak and fallible and selfish and perverse in some proportion. We intend and forget. We promise and do not deliver. We propose and do not pursue. We barely manage to camouflage our pettiness and our touchiness about our little empires. We see creations of deli-

The New Testament As Personal Reading

cacy gobbled up by the ravages of passion. The more we know about our motives the more shabby some of them are revealed to be. If we have to get all of that right before God accepts us we are without hope.

They say that symbols and myths about evil are among the most pervasive in world-literature. It is not surprising: a sense of weakness and failure (and ultimately of death) are among the most primordial of our experiences. There are other facets to us, of course: this is only the shadow side; this Jack, joke, poor potsherd is immortal diamond. But there *is* this and it could be depressing, if we couldn't meet it. Paul found it depressing and asked to be delivered from it. There is mystery here in this valley where moral striving, failure and forgiveness meet. It is a territory in which some of our storytellers — secular and religious — have made more exciting raids on the inarticulate than has our formal theology. One of the earliest stories is this:

> Now the serpent was more subtle than any other wild creature that the Lord God had made. He said to the woman, 'Did God say, "You shall not eat of any tree of the garden"?' . . . She took of its fruit and ate; and she also gave to her husband and he ate. Then the eyes of both were opened, and they knew that they were naked . . .

That is one way of dealing with the reality. Our New Testament story seems to me to face the same issue. It is better, more personal, more hopeful.

> He also told this parable to some who trusted in themselves that they were righteous and despised others: 'Two men went up into the temple to pray, one a pharisee and the other a tax-collec-

tor. The pharisee stood and prayed thus with himself. "God, I thank thee that I am not like other men, extortioners, unjust, adulterers, or even like this tax-collector. I fast twice a week. I give tithes of all that I get." But the tax-collector, standing far off would not even lift his eyes to heaven, but beat his breast, saying, "God, be merciful to me a sinner." I tell you, this man went down to his house justified rather than the other . . .'

It so happens that this year I saw three plays each of which in its own way set me thinking further along these lines. I feel carried into a cosmic solidarity in sin by the quiet line of the doctor in *Macbeth*, seeing that troubled lady: 'God, forgive us all.' The great issue came back again as Vanya surveyed the wasteland of his life. ('If only I could wake some still bright morning and feel that life had begun again; that the past was forgotten and had vanished like smoke. Oh, to begin life anew . . .') There are biblical songs and stories that meet that kind of bleakness with quiet hope. There were awkward echoes, too, in Helmer's unloving judgement (*A Doll's House*) on his wife's loving foolishness — the kind of relentless flaying of weakness that only the spuriously holy can quite muster. It left me wondering about our moral judgements, about the climate of our ministry of forgiveness and about the perfect love that casts out fear. (Father, I missed Mass . . . and I'm not sure if I told my sins right in my last confession . . . and I'm worried about confessions when I was younger . . . and is it a sin to — we all remember our youthful, and not so youthful, anxieties.) One meets priests who find hearing confessions depressing not because it is boring but because of the humiliating scavenging for sin in the rag-bag of the

The New Testament As Personal Reading

heart over which they have to preside. Most of us were afraid to trust the parables as much as we trusted the rules — although our instincts told us otherwise. If we find ourselves almost redundant in that area, it is not entirely our own fault. A revolt of heart and imagination was required but it was fitful and easily put down.

It sometimes seems to me that some branches of the Reformed tradition are more kindly and gentle than are Roman Catholics. Is there a hardness about us that comes from being assured from youth that we — the Church, of course, not we personally (as if there were a difference!) — have always been in the right, that we have proprietorship of the truth and responsibility for the good? The kindliness comes, perhaps, from a greater admission in their theology of the sinfulness and weakness of human kind. If your theology is constructed on the forgiveness of God, you cannot afford to be judgemental. 'Be kind to one another, tender-hearted, forgiving, as God in Christ forgave you' (Eph. 4:32). 'Why do you see the mote in your brother's eye and cannot see the beam in your own?' (Matt. 7:3). 'You shall not wrong a stranger or oppress him, for you were strangers in the land of Egypt' (Ex. 22:21). The forgiveness of God has ethical implications for us.

Ethical life could, indeed, be seen as a response to forgiveness. One of the most inspiring pieces of ethical writing I have read (though it does not set out to be such) is Joachim Jeremias's little piece on the Sermon on the Mount. His point is that if we read the Sermon on its own we have torn it out of its total perspective. Every word of the Sermon, he says, was preceded by something else. It was preceded by the preaching of the kingdom of God: 'You are forgiven,

Waiting on God

you are a child of God, you belong to the kingdom.' It is as if to every saying of the Sermon (so Jeremias puts it) we are first to supply, 'your sins are forgiven': therefore, because your sins are forgiven, there now follows, 'While you are still in the way with your opponent, be reconciled to him quickly.' Because 'Your sins are forgiven', there now follows, 'Love your enemies, and pray for those who persecute you' . . . And so on. The same dynamic comes across in the story of the wicked servant: 'I forgave you all that debt because you besought me; and should not you have had mercy on your fellow-man, as I have mercy on you?' (Matt. 18:37). To know who you are before God, warts and all, is a healthy state and if it does not depress it can refine. There is wisdom in Yeat's prayer that his daughter would not be too beautiful.

> For such
> being made beautiful overmuch
> consider beauty a sufficient end,
> Lose natural kindness . . .
> In courtesy I'd have her chiefly learned:
> Hearts are not had as a gift but hearts are earned
> By those that are not entirely beautiful . . .

I have often pondered on what one might call the problem of the ethical God, on the theological concept of punishment and on (what seems to be closely connected with it) the loss of faith among young people. I have rooted around in the neo-Scholastic manuals which have been a major influence on our catechisms and on our popular religious consciousness. Some of what I have found has been horrific and it is as well that it was tempered by a more benign devotional writing and pastoral practice. Take this paraphrase of the very influential moral philosopher, Cathrein.

The New Testament As Personal Reading

Law, he says (as does almost every other philosopher and theologian of the period) requires a sanction: if God wished his moral law to be kept the only way for him to do it was to impose reward and punishment for it; only the eternal punishment of hell or reward of heaven would be a sufficient stimulus; to impose a lesser punishment would be contrary to the wisdom of God. It would be hard to overestimate the influence which that has had on our idea of God. It has largely created the Roman Catholic subconscious. It is at the root of our most basic fears and hopes and expectations. It *is* many people's conception of God. Why didn't someone sprinkle in even a pinch of the Aquinas who says that there is no hope of justification in the commandments as such, but in faith alone (In 1 Tim. lect. 3)?

I have wandered into dangerous terrain — justification, no less — and some forward scout of orthodoxy may well pick me off. However, as I said, one can record some thaw in this theology of deterrence. One finds theologians trying to right the picture, saying that faith does not imply a religious performance by which one attempts to please God but an abandonment of any performance on man's part and an admission that he can do nothing himself (Böckle). Or that the purpose for which man must discern good and evil and govern himself is not to secure God's welcome, which is assured him in any case (Burtchaell). Not to mention Küng's major contribution and Rahner's large agreement with him. The roll-call is simply to give some kind of — well, if not theological justification, at least some backing — to my tentativeness here and to what I know is the instinct of others.

What I am trying to point up is that we are to iden-

Waiting on God

tify ourselves as a community of those who are by definition weak and failing and who acknowledge and accept one another as such. ('I confess to Almighty God . . . and to you, my brothers and sisters, that I have sinned . . . And I ask blessed Mary ever virgin . . . and you, my brothers and sisters, to pray for me . . .') People who know that they have been accepted by God as such. The glory of us is that we believe together that the ultimate reality is forgiving. We may not be able to forgive ourselves, others may not forgive us, history may not forgive us. But God does — and not conditionally. It is not only if we have first shined and combed ourselves and put on our best suits and made ourselves respectable enough to appear in his presence that he does so. He does it anyway. The ultimate sin, as the parable tells us, is to think that you are somebody, to trust yourself, to count up, to confuse Christianity with knowing that you have done right. Everything is gift and grace and acceptance. It could be that we would never learn that. It is a hard saying of Jesus to those who sit on the chair of Moses that the harlots are nearer to the kingdom than they are. We are never nearer to the kingdom than when together, prelate and pensioner, we recognize that we are all in need of acceptance and forgiveness, that we have received it and that this is cause for common celebration. I don't think we have enough of it in the Church, although the reform of the rite of penance is slowly inching towards it. 'God, have mercy on Bartley's soul and on Michael's soul and on the souls of Shamus and Patch and on Stephen and Shaun and may he have mercy on my soul, Nora, and on the soul of every one who is left living in this world.'

'Has no man condemned you, woman?' (No man is

The New Testament As Personal Reading

in a position to condemn when his own sins are written on the ground.) 'Neither will I.' Jesus gets things into focus for that little gospel group. He did not accuse anyone. He simply let them remember together their humanity and their shared condition before God. That was enough to induce some reticence and to make an unloving zeal for the law look foolish. Jesus had a way of subverting received ideas. You won't get me wrong, I know. I am not making a pitch for bigger and better sins. On the contrary: 'Your sins are forgiven', therefore 'while you are still in the way with your opponent . . .' What I say is not meant to be depressing but liberating. I am trying to feel my way about God and loving-mercy (*hesed*) and about the gentleness and freedom that come from a common recognition of our flawed beauty. I am concerned about the remark of Vatican II that we are sometimes responsible for the atheism of others. I am wondering about the image of the Church and about signs of credibility:

> For I will leave in the midst of you
> a people humble and lowly.
> They shall seek refuge in the name
> of the Lord . . .
> For they shall pasture and lie down
> and none shall make them afraid (Zeph. 3:11).

I am chewing over: 'For it is by his grace you are saved, through trusting him; it is not your own doing. It is God's gift, not a reward for work done. There is nothing for anyone to boast of' (Eph. 2:8). As I said, there is mystery here and I have not got my theological act fully together. I don't think anyone can. We have so many stories about God, so many skeins of

Waiting on God

our tribal heritage — not to be worked into some neat and easy pattern. I am only saying that we should dwell on this one more and tell it oftener around the firesides of our hearts. It is a simple tale but it cracks open fundamental issues for us. It was the one who recognized his limitations and failures who went down to his house justified rather than the other (who told no lie but who either had not lived long enough or had not learned much from life). In the end, it is more important for us to get it right with the publican than with the pharisee. We are to wait on the Lord and count on his word. We are to remember that:

> Sin is Behovely, but
> All shall be well, and
> All manner of thing shall be well.

That, as they say, is the bottom line for us.

At Cross Purposes
Jesus and the Disciples in Mark

Seán Freyne

At one point only in the gospel of Mark does the author step out from behind the anonymity that shrouds most creative writers, ancient and modern, and address his readers directly. 'Let the reader understand', is his warning signal to us as he describes the apocalyptic cataclysm with which the history of the present evil age is to be concluded (13:14). Unfortunately for the correct reading of Mark, this address has been taken more seriously by those who seek in the Scriptures a detailed calendar of the end-time, than by the more general run of Christians looking to this and other New Testament writings for a message of hope and a way of living in the present. It is unfortunate, because it obscures an important facet of the work that was certainly part of the author's intention (since it is the intention of every creative writer who puts pen to paper) namely, to address a wider readership through the characters, episodes and plot around which the story is built. The good story teller will allow the characters to speak for him or her. Emphases, interests and values are made to emerge indirectly, through the portrayal of individuals interacting with each other and giving the plot its thrust forward to a final *dénouement*. They do the speaking for the writer, whose creativity emerges in the ability to make them real-life people, capable of engaging us, the readers, in their tensions and struggles, yet also challenging us to see things differently — either because of the ideals they embody as the story unfolds, or through the shock we receive from their

Seán Freyne is Professor of Theology at Trinity College, Dublin.

At Cross Purposes

unexpected and strange reactions to events or circumstances as they occur. We must be able to identify with them, yet recognize our distance, if we are to experience the purifying effects that Aristotle, dealing with tragedy, describes as pity and fear, but which, I take it, can cover a whole range of other emotions also, depending on the nature of the story.

MARK AS STORY TELLER

These introductory reflections on the role of the writer in good story-telling are particularly apposite when the message is as strange, as important and as difficult to communicate as is that of Mark. Because his message touches the heart of a resistant human condition, his strategies have to combine the skills of the good narrator with the gifts of the dramatist, amusing, shocking and enthralling us, at once. That Mark was aware of his task and equal to its demands can be seen on almost every page of his work. Perhaps nothing exemplifies it better than the aura of mystery that pervades the whole, the strange secrecy that cloaks everything in obscurity, particularly those events and symbols that are meant to be revealing. 'Do you not understand this parable? How will you understand all the parables?' 'They did not understand about the loaves, their hearts were hardened.' 'So they kept the matter to themselves, questioning what the rising from the dead meant.' These and other comments which our author subtly inserts into his narrative, keep us, the readers on tenterhooks about the outcome, yet push us to take a stance within the unfolding plot. They are questions that draw us into the story, so that we ourselves are, in the end, questioned by the whole. We can no longer remain neutral about the outcome, because we recognize that our own destiny is somehow bound up with its conclusion.

The New Testament As Personal Reading

Apart from the central character Jesus, the disciples are easily the most developed of Mark's *personae dramatis*. They clearly are intended as a backdrop against which the author can develop the contours of the Jesus figure he wishes to portray. Indeed, the strangeness of Jesus only emerges against the peculiar features of the disciples' presentation. The paradox that is his person is matched by the unpredictability of their reactions, ranging from blind acceptance of his call to follow him to abandoning him in his hour of crisis (1:16-20; 14:50). Other groups and characters within the story are important in various ways for its development. Jewish religious leaders, the Herodians and Pilate are essential if the plot is to reach its intended climax; the crowd, in the role of an awkward but benign mob, form the appropriate, comic backdrop, as the blocking character that must be circumvented, if the real action is to progress (cf. 1:45; 9, 20; 4:1; 5:24, 31; 6:33, 45; 7:33; 8:23); the demons are used to highlight the intensity of the struggle in which Jesus is engaged and form a striking contrast to all humans, except the centurion, in their readiness to confess Jesus as Son (Holy One) of God (1:24; 3:11; 5, 7); other individuals, named and unnamed, such as Bar Timaeus, the centurion and the Gadarene demoniac, help to bring the disciple's failures into clearer focus, and can be contrasted with the leader of the group, Peter and the betrayer Judas, in that 'outsiders' become 'insiders' and those 'within' either align themselves with the enemies of Jesus (Judas, 14:10f) or are in danger of doing so (Peter, 8:33). Thus, all groups and individuals in Mark's narrative can be defined in terms of their relationship with or contrast to the disciples. This is wholly understandable, for already at the time of writing, 'disciple' had become a technical term for believer in early Christian parlance, and Mark's immediate gaze is focussed

At Cross Purposes

not so much backwards to the historical companions of the earthly Jesus as forward to all those who might wish to describe themselves by such a name. Mark knew that his readers were, and would continue to be, Christians, and it is these, as the implied readers, that he wishes to address in his story about Jesus.

Mark has often been described as a clumsy writer, not really in control of his material. This, it is sometimes alleged, explains not just awkward and inelegant Greek (largely lost in modern translation) but other features also, such as interruptions in telling stories like the raising of the ruler's daughter in chapter 5 and the mission of the twelve in chapter 6; climaxes such as 8:29, that prove to be pointless as the story progresses, or commands to silence that cannot reasonably be expected to be observed, and instead seem to generate the very opposite effect to what was intended (cf. e.g. 1:45; 7:36f). These, and other apparent anomalies within the text should not be dismissed so easily as the signs of an artless construction, but rather as a challenge to us not to seek to impose our order on the work, thereby missing its real impact. When, as readers, we respond to that challenge, we find that the very passages and aspects that before did not fit are now parts that help to build up the puzzle of the whole — the contrasts, the apparent contradictions, the strangeness and surprising features of many of the characters, above all the mysterious non-ending that leaves us to supply our own (as some early Christians did, borrowing from the later writers) — all these facets of the text help to achieve the overall effect that Mark sought, and we must allow them their full impact. In the end we are left with the great riddle for 'outsiders', that is so 'unreal' as to merit the description 'mystery' for 'insiders' (4:11f), and yet can be encapsulated in short story of loss, leading to gain (4:2-9) — a

The New Testament As Personal Reading

play within a play that, like *Hamlet's* third act, gives the key to the meaning of the whole.

CALLED BUT BLIND

It is in the opening section of the second half of the gospel (8:31-10:52) that Mark really shows the disciples at *cross*-purposes with Jesus, as the title of this article — supplied by the editor, incidentally (!) — so cleverly suggests. However, it is important not to isolate this particular section from the portrayal elsewhere, since the disciples are at the centre of the action in the first half of the gospel also. They emerge at the very opening of the public ministry where the call of Jesus to the first four disciples and their prompt response is deliberately juxtaposed with the initial proclamation of the kingdom (1:14f and 1:16-20). At the outset the reader is given a yardstick by which to measure their subsequent reactions and this initial call is subsequently reinforced by a second call that links discipleship with membership of the Twelve, that is, God's new messianic people (3:13-14). Here, 'following' is replaced, at least temporarily, by 'being with him' as the hallmark of the disciple, but its non-elitist character is made clear by the use of two terms that are descriptive of early Christian outreach — 'to be sent' and 'to preach'. This particular scene comes immediately after one in which Mark depicts a huge crowd coming to Jesus from all the different regions of Palestine. Yet, the attentive reader cannot but be struck by the curious contrast that is tantamount to a withdrawal by Jesus 'to those whom he would himself', and that, despite the hint of future mission that is suggested in the language used to describe the election of the Twelve.

This impression of separation is further confirmed

At Cross Purposes

by the two episodes that immediately follow the election. In the Beelzebul controversy 'his own', namely, his mother and his brothers, are left outside the house while inside are the disciples and the opponents, but the two locations represent spiritual and psychological attitudes rather than physical proximity: 'for they said he is beside himself'. The parable chapter (chapter 4) continues the idea of locative separation as a symbol of deeper divisions, by making the house the place of interpretation and 'outside' the place for crowd instruction, who are addressed in parables, 'according as they were able to understand'. Whereas 'privately' he explained everything to his own disciples (4:33f). At the beginning of the chapter another more mobile object of separation had come into play, namely the boat (4:1), which previously had been ordered to be made ready 'because of the crowd, lest they crush him' (3:9). The separation has deeper theological roots, however, for, to those inside the mystery of the kingdom of God has been given, whereas to those outside 'everything happens in riddles' (4:11f). We are now in a much better position to understand why the shift from 'following' to 'being with him' as descriptive of authentic discipleship had taken place — following is not intended to be blind obedience but the result of deep understanding that is given rather than acquired. Neither Mark nor his first readers felt the need to apologise for divine favours — they are simply assumed, not argued, so strong was the sense of election that they both cherished.

The parable chapter had not specified the content of the mystery, yet for those with eyes to see and ears to hear, the three parables — like stories within the story — had given the key to the whole and prepared for what was to come: when all seemed lost, scattered

The New Testament As Personal Reading

seed produced unexpected and extraordinary return; seed that is sown leads to the harvest in its own time and in a way that man can neither control nor comprehend; insignificant and tiny seeds produce great and protective trees. Three times the seed is sown and three times the clues are given, but unavailingly, it would seem. The boat (4:35; 5:21; 6:32, 45; 8:14) reappears and disciples experience Jesus as Lord of the Deep (4:35-41; 6:45-51) and feeder of thousands in the desert (6:37-43; 8:1-10), but with little understanding of the significance of any of these events. They are terrified; their hearts are hardened; they can only recall the externals; how do they not yet understand? Nothing has penetrated, or so it would seem, as Act One draws to a close with the most cryptic of all healings — a blind man has his eyes opened in *two* stages, so that he was able to see 'everything clearly' (8:22-26). The time has come for the first real test of discipleship, and to the unwary reader Peter would seem to have passed with flying colours: 'But you, whom do you say that I am?', to which Peter answers: 'You are the Christ' (8:29). Yet, despite the apparent breakthrough enough has been said to indicate that this confession was not adequate and that more was yet to come. Twice, the failure in understanding had been described, following Old Testament precedents, as not seeing (4:12; 8:18) and the two-stage cure of the blind man made the point dramatically, if somewhat elusively. The stern warning to Peter not to make Jesus' identity known (8:30), couched as it is in the language with which demons were addressed earlier, could scarcely leave any doubt in the reader's mind that not merely was the 'confession' of Peter inadequate, it could possibly share something of the sinister power of the enemy, and so Peter had to be si-

At Cross Purposes

lenced. Stern stuff indeed, and enough to keep the audience on their toes for what was to follow, even if they had not fully shared Mark's palpable frustration at the lack of comprehension and blindness of the disciples.

THE WAY OF RELUCTANT FOLLOWING

'Being with him' suggests a rather static relationship, that in the end had failed to stretch the disciples' understanding. That Mark wished to return to the more dynamic, if demanding description of 'following' is hinted at in the opening verses of Act Two. Jesus, as he is about to rebuke Peter for rejecting the idea of a suffering Son of man, turns and sees the other disciples; already there is the suggestion that Jesus has gone ahead, and this impression is confirmed by Mark's repeated use of 'the way' motif in this section pointing to a straggling bunch of reluctant disciples, following Jesus at some distance (cf. 10:32). Like several other words of early Christian self-description, the term 'way' had a number of different resonances — Israel's journeyings in the desert; the ethical standards that the movement subscribed to and expected of its members — and the first readers would have thought of their own commitments in these perspectives also. But Mark wishes to deepen and clarify such associations, and so, as Jesus moves from the northern borders of Galilee to Jerusalem, references to the way are sprinkled liberally throughout the narrative, and the object of the journey becomes more specific as it gets nearer to its goal. The question to Peter was put 'on the way' at Caesarea Philippi, just after a blind man had been restored to full sight (8:27), and the section ends with another blind man, also restored to sight, following Jesus 'on the way' (10:52).

The New Testament As Personal Reading

Mark wishes to link the motif of the way with that of seeing: one can only properly embark on the way when one clearly sees and accepts the outcome to which it leads. This is specified as 'the way to Jerusalem' (10:32) or 'his way' (10:17), as though it has become synonymous in advance with Jesus' fate in the holy city. It thus takes on a sacral character for the reader, a genuinely sacred way, that, it transpires, is also a *via dolorosa*, since Mark suitably signposts it with three predictions of the death and resurrection of the Son of Man (8:31; 9:30; 10:32). It is all the more incongruous, therefore, that the disciples behave in a highly inappropriate manner 'on the way' at 9:33f, where they have been discussing the question of rank among themselves, a singularly unsuitable topic for such a setting, as Mark will make clear.

The predictions of the suffering and rising Son of man are signposts to the way, we have suggested, and Mark has made them stand out so clearly that no attentive reader could miss the sad irony that surrounds them. The first signposting is prompted by Peter's declaration 'you are the Christ' and his subsequent silencing. A new and strange description for Jesus introduces the section, totally ignoring the Christian title used by Peter: *The Son of man* must suffer, die and on the third day rise again. 'And he said this plainly' (8:32) — a rather striking contrast to the silence that had just been enjoined and the parabolic and symbolic character of the earlier communications. Peter rejects any such idea of suffering, however, obviously quite unaffected by the response to his previous utterance. The reply of Jesus is swift and incisive: Peter is said to be aligned with Satan, merely for thinking human thoughts, and his attitudes are clearly seen as having a detrimental effect on all the

At Cross Purposes

disciples. However, the clarification to follow excludes nobody, since suddenly the 'insider' 'outsider' division of the first act disappears. Disciples and crowd can be summoned together to hear the invitation that is open to all: 'if *any man* will come after me, let him deny himself, take up his cross and follow me' (8:34). There is no need to be cryptic about such a message since it is based on the most startling paradox imaginable — saving one's life is achieved only through losing it. This is so strange that there is almost a touch of black comedy about calling it gospel or good news, but that is precisely what Mark does! This pattern of prediction, totally inappropriate reaction of disciples or their representatives and striking clarification by Jesus will repeat itself at the second and third signposts along the way, conscious as Mark is of the fact that his good news is so foreign to the expectations or even the horizons of understanding of his readership. Cumulative effect may be achieved by repetition, even if understanding cannot be expected before journey's end.

The second prediction (9:30f) varies from the first only in detail; the message is the same. For disciples concerned about 'which of them is the greatest' such incidentals could scarcely have any consequence, however. Understandably, in the light of the first prediction, the privacy of earlier sections is restored: 'He was passing through Galilee and he would not have anyone know it', but even this circumstance can scarcely inspire confidence in view of the new variation on the theme to be elaborated: 'If anyone would be first he must be last of all and servant of all'. The presence of a child as an illustration of what this might mean could not soften such a harsh saying for those whose eyes and ears are still closed, and Mark,

The New Testament As Personal Reading

the master of the concrete picture, will shortly inform us that the disciples rebuked those who brought up little children to Jesus (10:13). Concrete reminders of what one does not want to hear are particularly threatening, yet they have an unhappy knack of turning up at the wrong time and in the most compromising of circumstances! Mark's sense of humour has not totally deserted him even in the midst of such human failings, nor does he wish to deny his readers at least a wry smile even in these awesome surroundings, provided of course they too do not share the disciples' attitudes.

The way has now become clearly focussed on Jerusalem as we reach the third signpost, and the dreaded message is heard yet again: the Son of man must suffer. . . . This time it is the opportunity of the other two members of the inner triumvirate, James and John, to demonstrate just how much Jesus and the disciples have been at cross-purposes from the start. They ask to sit on his right and his left in his glory (10:37) but with little understanding of what is implied in such a request. With another touch of his black comedy Mark will later relate that two thieves were crucified with Jesus one on his left hand and the other on his right (15:27), and even if the reader cannot be expected to see the ironic contrast at the earlier episode, the image of 'drinking from my chalice' that Jesus introduces in his response, certainly gives their request to be seated with him in glory, a new and slightly sinister aspect. The reader will not be overly impressed by the indignation of the ten in view of their earlier performance, and again the whole issue has to be clarified with a third image of reversal — those who aspire to being greatest must beome servants of all, following the example of the servant

At Cross Purposes

Jesus, 'who gives his life as a ransom for many' (10:45). This indeed is service beyond the call of duty, and if they are ever going to aspire to such an ideal there is need for further eye opening prior to its enactment in Jerusalem. This time there are no two stages to the cure: 'And immediately he received his sight and followed him on the way' (10:52).

This final scene, the cure of the blind Bar Timaeus, stands in sharp contrast to an earlier one, the transfiguration story and before we enter Jerusalem it is worth pausing to ponder the implications. The inner group of disciples are taken up the mountain, and granted a vision whereas Bar Timaeus asks for sight; Jesus is clothed in other-worldly garments, but the blind man is prepared to abandon his; Peter's attitude in proposing three tabernacles is not shared by the blind man, eager to move on as he springs up and comes to Jesus; his 'son of David' plea may be but a pale echo of the Father's declaration about his beloved son, but it clearly rings more true than Peter's call 'teacher', or his 'Christ'-confession, earlier. What is it about these insiders who are so afraid in the presence of the transfigured Master when an outsider can approach him with such confidence and openness? Election to insider status clearly brings its own peculiar risks because it generates false expectations — that make it particularly difficult to see real possibilities, as distinct from empty hopes and unfulfillable dreams. One can only receive in accordance with the measure one brings, and if that measure is already full then nothing can be given, least of all the 'still more' that is promised for those to whom the mystery is given (4:24). If the disciple is to receive any rewards it is only 'with persecution' (10:30), because Jesus is the model and he was prepared to lose his life, be least of all and be slave of all, none of which is compatible with the expectation of personal gains and rewards.

The reader may not have made these formal connections between the two stories, but he can hardly be left in any doubt about the risks of discipleship and the challenge it poses to normal human ways of thinking and acting. We cannot stay on the Jericho road, we must enter as part of the procession to see if anything has been achieved by this intense section of instruction either for the disciples themselves, or possibly for us the readers through them. How will they and we react to the events that lie ahead? Before we are critical of them let us join them in their trial.

JERUSALEM AND BEYOND

They share Jesus' entry into Jerusalem and are present as he privately inspects the temple (11:11), which his death will replace as the true place of meeting with God, according to Mark (cf. 14:58; 15:38). The four who were originally called and responded so promptly in chapter 1 are given a final message of hope for the elect, to prepare them for the coming crisis (13:3), yet when that hour does come three of these very disciples, though asked to stay with Jesus in his agony, fall asleep, and they do not know how to answer when he confronts them with their lack of concern. But worse is to follow. One of them will betray him, another will deny him when a girl from his homeland suggests that he was 'with him' (!), cursing and swearing his innocence of such a charge. Mark sums it up in one sombre statement: 'Then the disciples all deserted him and fled' (14:50). If their performance 'on the way' was less than becoming, that in Jerusalem was dismal indeed. It clearly is not their kind of place and before he was finally separated from them, Jesus suggested that they should all meet again in Galilee (14:28). Their absence at the final tragic moment when it was left to an outsider to recognize him for what he really was, something the reader too can recognize (cf. 1:1; 1:11; 9:7), still does not invalidate the initial call in Galilee. Hopefully, they received the final message and acted on it: 'Go tell his disciples and Peter that he will go before you to Galilee'. There they will see him as he told them (16:7).

Were Mark to write the happy ending that some early Christians felt he should have (cf. 16:9-20, which must be seen as a later addition not from the hand of our author), he would have destroyed the effect which he has striven to create from the start. He has hurried us along to this point and now when we reach the empty tomb Jesus is already gone ahead again to Galilee. Should the disciples and we accept the invitation to return there, we are given an assurance that we will see him. Perhaps then we will be able to follow more confidently in the way, as companions of the blind Bar Timaeus. Hopefully, the stories of the Galilean ministry will reassure us now that he is Lord of the Storm, even when he appears to sleep and the boat is tossed about, and that he can feed us in the desert with broken pieces as he gives thanks. Will we be able to remember properly, now at least, and celebrate his presence in the midst of death and evil and failure? Our seeing him in Galilee for what he really is will only be possible if we have at least learned from the centurion's seeing him for what he truly was at the moment of his supreme failure (15:39). Mark's drama will then not just be a fleeting catharsis of our pity and fear as we return to the everyday, but a powerful message of hope, and a chal-

The New Testament As Personal Reading

lenge to find him in the midst of an everyday that is signed with the sign of death. Surely it is a story that bears re-telling in our time.

SUGGESTED FURTHER READING:

S. Freyne, *Mark, Scripture Discussion Commentary*, no. 7. Sheed and Ward 1972.
W. Kelber, *Mark's Story of Jesus*, Fortress 1979.
F. Kermode, *The Genesis of Secrecy*, Harvard University Press, 1979.
N. R. Petersen (ed.), *Perspectives on Mark's Gospel*. Semeia vol. 16 Scholars' Press, 1980.

The Olive Tree in the Forum
— the Letter to the Romans

Seán Quinlan

Nature has good taste. For that reason, you will be forgiven if you were offended on seeing some years ago, and perhaps they still survive, *graffiti* from St Paul daubed in whitewash on the rocks on that lovely road from Killarney to Kenmare: as if creation, in that sweet fellowship of sandstone, fern and saxifrage, needed further proof of God's *fiat* at the beginning.

In cities, too, as you look through bus windows, you see big hoardings proclaim, between advertisements for automobiles and Scotch, that 'The wages of sin is death', *Romans* 6:23, and 'Christ died for the ungodly', *Romans* 5:6. Almost always the same texts.

They stare at you from the frigid isolation of print, lone rangers armed with menace. You do not doubt the message, but you tremble, more or less, at the monomania.

That is Paul: the commando about to stride through Sodom and Gomorrah at midnight, and then sit down at dawn at his writing table, the gloomy dean of *Romans*. And patron saint of male chauvinists to boot. Or so it seems.

You may also have heard that the hoardings are all financed by oil tycoons in Texas. Largely a myth, I suspect; more likely with the pennies and cents of obscure and humble people, who mean well but live in a penumbra of fear, where shade and light do not blend.

But it is, at least, a fear with a name to it: it's not

Seán Quinlan is a priest of the diocese of Kerry. He is Professor of New Testament at St Patrick's College, Maynooth.

The New Testament As Personal Reading

that wraith called *Angst,* the notifiable soul disease, *par excellence,* of our time: a thing dissected for years in academic laboratories and bandaged up, more or less, with dissertations. For Paul it has a name, and it is palpable in everything from toothache to death: *the mystery of iniquity.* And Paul believed that the blood of Christ had penetrated the darkness of iniquity as rain sinks into parched earth and releases hapless seeds to life and light. The tragic name found meaning and the whole human vocabulary of pain and death was bound in one volume by crucified and glorious flesh. Aeschylus and Dante merge in a single reading. The title of the volume is *Resurrection.*

But the hoardings still gleam like permafrost on granite. The entrepreneurs, however, are not entirely consistent. From time to time, those half country cousins of *Romans,* the *Epistles to the Corinthians* are quoted instead: 'In Christ God was reconciling the world to himself', 2 *Corinthians* 5:19. Immediately you are surprised by joy. You know that such a cosmic sweep by God can scarcely leave you unknown to Christ and that in spite of yourself you will be compelled to him.

The starkness of the hoardings seems to be due to a flaw in us. We tend to make points too strongly by isolating powerful expressions when Bible texts should always be read in the neighbourhood of other Bible texts. Christ must enter us through many pores and without a stop watch. The too powerful light needs a correcting shadow and the deep shadow needs a correcting light.

The Bible is portraiture: God, Christ, man. We need multi-focal vision. And we should not hear it monophonically. We need stereo for its counterpoint.

We have another flaw. The stark and the ominous

The Olive Tree in the Forum

are news, and news is the untranquil part of us. An earthquake, which is abnormal, is more obvious than a flower growing quietly, or an infant sleeping. There are more infants and flowers than there are earthquakes.

Sin is more strident than love. Love, like good weather, we take for granted. Yet, love is the depth in the texture of all that is. Sin is skiff, love is anchor. Love has no worldly power. Love has a homely face.

And it's on these lines we have to follow Paul, to the village of his heart.

We have another, an educated flaw. We tend to read Paul as if he were a university man writing in timeless style, and not as a Mediterranean man of a nervous temperament who was, like Our Lord and John, a poet. And a man subject to the tremors of a great capacity for the fire in the depth of things.

The papal style, for instance, is Mediterranean, and, until recently, was always in danger of running out of superlatives. The danger now may be pontifical slang and Palestrina on the tin whistle.

Paul, the Mediterranean Jew, exaggerates. Love always exaggerates, not the way the powerful exaggerate, but rather as boys exaggerate as they watch their football team in action. Paul is polemical as well, a fairly inevitable twinship with love in certain conditions.

This man of the sun and the olive, the unimpressed neighbour of the Grecian urn, the soul edged by the anguish of Israel, the part fanatic startled and blinded by bloodstained light near Damascus, could never sound like the cracking of a match on wet stone. Besides, as a prophet and a genius, he had little talent for the agreeable compromise, although time did ease that somewhat.

The New Testament As Personal Reading

There is in him a melancholic streak. He does not lend himself to the glossy print, but then life is more than beer and charismatic skittles. We are exiles, and a certain Christian sadness is an imperative for spiritual refinement in life.

Judging him by his maturity in *Philippians,* one is drawn to say that the poet in him must have begun to serve the believer in him ever since, *jung und morgensh8on,* he will have watched the cranes fly over Tarsus. They still do.

He will then have moved on to that point in youth where religion and art, that theology of the less than the eternal — begin the long meditation on lost innocence. Between then and his death, he is the Jewish super-zealot, intense, sincere, before he crosses the rift valley between Judaism and the cross, without ever ceasing to look back towards the other side and his own traditions sculptured there by God.

He then becomes apprentice, journeyman, and master tailor, cutting for himself, and for us, the garment of the innocence of Christ, which is not a garment but pure and eternal nakedness, since there is no cold.

Paul is a modest, magnanimous and very affectionate man. In *Romans* he greets Andronicus and Junias, who 'were in Christ before me', and Epaenetus, 'first convert in Asia for Christ', and Rufus, whose mother is 'my mother too'.

He is a joyful man. In the New Testament as a whole the word 'joy' occurs 59 times in all, 21 are in Paul. The verb 'rejoice', 74 times in all, 29 in Paul. Less often in *Romans* than in the earlier *Corinthians* or in the later *Philippians*. *Philippians* is the last testament, full of quiet joy.

The word 'grace' which is shorthand for God's sin—

The Olive Tree in the Forum

gle-minded pre-occupation with love for us occurs 155 times in the New Testament as a whole, 100 in Paul.

On the other hand, 'wrath' totals 36, and 26 of these are in Paul and 5 only in the four gospels. Still 'joy' and 'grace' outnumber 'wrath' by eight to one.

And when you ask who the champion is when it comes to the great word, 'love', most people will say John. Not so. Another example of the dominating power of the isolated text. Noun and verb together, it's Paul 108, John 43, but allowing for the differing proportion of text in each the best thing is to declare it a draw. They were not competing. In Paul 'love' and 'grace' and 'joy' are substance, 'wrath' is a warning sign.

In fact, 'wrath', as a careful reading of *Romans* 1:24-32 will show, is man's own self when he abandons God and becomes a minion of that 'secret force of lawlessness', 2 *Thessalonians* 2:7.

Paul lived in a brutal age. The war of the Four Emperors is almost contemporaneous with *Romans* and he lived full in the middle of that degraded society that fed the *saeva indignatio* of the classical satirists.

I have no great fear of nuclear warfare. That's not courage. Rather, it's a form of self-indulgence since I am not far from the chimney nook and have no family. But when I see (*Sunday Times*, 8 November 1981), at the end of the week when we heard of 'contingency plans to fire a nuclear weapon as a demonstration in Europe'; when I see Nato troops with octopus eyes in anti-neutron and anti-chemical helmets, I shudder at the thought of children and sweet-hearts and all the kind and tender things on earth.

Compared to all that, Wilfred Owen's (*obiit*, 4 November 1918) 'passing bells for those who die as cat-

The New Testament As Personal Reading

tle', seems almost a peace. Like Paul, the poet warned. But compared with these new lethal immensities of man's making Paul seems a mere scold.

If 10% of mankind had 1% of Paul's soul, we could hope that all that death would remain caged in impotence in the storage silos of his charity. Even without that, we may hope, the children and the sweet-hearts may still be saved by whatever Pauline flotsam and jetsam survives in the pools left behind by Sophocles' Aegean.

He wrote his most famous letter, the vane of so many theological storms, to the Roman Christians, living by the Forum, that stone hinge of law and force, of war and peace in the universe, that had grown up around the original consecrated trapezium, a small patch of soil that held only the staples of Mediterranean life: the vine, the fig, the olive. Paul, a Jew, a Roman citizen, the first Christian ambassador, an outsider. Nothing really significant ever happens in the colonies. Besides scorpions, there are some curiosities; Jewish memory, for instance; somewhat *outré*: Abraham, Moses, the Prophets, the Covenants, the Ark, the Menorah, and the Platonic quackery of Philo.

The pupils of Paul's eyes had been removed near Damascus. If you had faith and looked into the microscopic craters that remained, you would see Christ. Some blood on the irises; corneas and scleras fully Jewish.

He had a message for the Romans that knows no bounds. It is the revelaion of the intimate character of God. He uses a turgid kind of word, *righteousness*. He should, had he been a scholar at leisure, really have put a footnote here: cf. 2 *Corinthians* 2:17, 'a fragrance from life to life', and, *ibid.*, 4:6, 'For it is the

The Olive Tree in the Forum

God who said, "Let light shine out of darkness", who has shone in our hearts to give the light of the knowledge of the glory of God in the face of Christ'.

He asks them to take stock of the world they see around them. The Roman Christians will have known some highminded and earnest pagans: imperial officers, perhaps; competent like Trajan, still a boy in Spain; or meditative like the future Marcus Aurelius who was to die in Paul's own native province: men who dipped into the Greek tragedians and hunted the wild boar in November in Aprutium.

Paul admits as much. Man has a natural goodness in his heart and can know of God in the way of natural religion. But no one can close his eyes to the terrible degradation of the times (chapter 1).

'My fellow Jews say, "Fine. That all applies to Roman pagans and the rest. But we are insiders." I say to them, "You have God's law. Do you keep it? Have you listened to our prophets? A pagan with a conscience is ahead of you. You think you can manipulate God. You amass merits, and say, 'God, this is my *quid*, you must now give me your *quo*'." Face to face with God, and my fellow Jews fail to see it; we are worthless. We are stillborn until he moves us. I heard a phrase in Christian circles and I hope someone writes it down permanently, "We love because he loved us first." That's it in a nutshell. Before, during and afterwards, he has to be the enabler. Our famous *law* in fact only shows us what we should be and are not. It simply leaves us aware that we are still guilt-ridden. It's a womb without seed' (chapters 2-3).

'Christ frees us, Jews and Gentiles, no exceptions. It's his gift to us, an absolute bonus. And faith in Christ is the spring that releases it. In as far as I can put a finger on it all, God acted, it would appear, because of the utter devotion to God in Christ's life on earth.'

'If I may play with a paradox or a parable or one of these things, and I'll go at it gingerly and ask you not to regard it as the last word, I'll find myself saying something like this. When God saw someone, Christ, of course, acting divinely on earth — in another place I speak of "in the form of God" — he had to look again at the human race. And when we, on our side, look at the life of Christ, a circuit begins to complete itself, so to speak. We watch the cloud of unknowing disperse and we gradually glimpse something of the face of God.'

'God lets sins go in the past. He was simply stalling, so to speak. Wretched, isn't it, that one has to say, *so to speak,* so often. But that was not God's definitive stance. Things are now definitive. God stands fully clear in his character and demands in Christ. Faith in Christ is the be all and the end all. From now on, untied knots are our responsibility (chapter 3).

'My fellow Jews make a poor point. Was not Abraham, they say, rewarded by God? Didn't he have a *quid* for God's *quo*? It was on terms of the law therefore that God accepted Abraham. No. Circumcision is no hall-mark from the divine assayer's office. God met Abraham first in the bond of faith before the circumcision. Read your text. First things first, and then we can see where the law fits in. God — Faith — Abraham; as vertical as a ray of sun at noon.'

'We are engulfed in God's love. And this love is shown like this. Christ died for us when we had nothing to offer but the *fact* that we had nothing to offer. You could put it mildly and say all we had to offer was the still sad music of humanity. But how about the trammels, a word, by the way, that means a net with

The Olive Tree in the Forum

three holes, and we were always caught in one or the other of them, how about the trammels of the mystery of iniquity with its octopus eyes? Powerful, alluring, nulliparous. It holds us, always held us, whether by strangle-hold or our complicity.'

'Christ has cleaned it away. Can I give you an illustration? Suppose you killed a man's father and mother, wife and children before his eyes, and then held a knife to his heart and plunged it in. Imagine him telling you before he died that he forgave you, that he had no shred of anger or bitterness in the ravelled fibres of his heart towards you. The thought is absurd. Well, in Christ it's not. And here we are on a universal level: all sin, all time, all mankind. They say that in *Romans* I'm too solemn, and that I have put the word of God in winter quarters. But you must have noticed there how I call God. *Abba*, the kind of affectionate word a little girl might use when her doting grandfather tousles her hair. That's because Christ has taken me, and you, into the very heart of the family; Christ, eternally *simpatico*.

'Jesus, the Jew, knew the depths of family ties in Israel, the obligation of the *goel*, the kinsman bound to redeem his kin in any distress. Jesus, the Christ, has given us a blood transfusion with his own blood against the RH negative of iniquity.'

'Think of it in terms of all mankind. Make the endless calculations of a Babylonian astronomer and you will still be as far as ever from grasping the endless love of Christ. Once among school children, Herodian's children were there, I said it was like comparing a single feather on a fallen sparrow to tens and tens of thousands of Jacob's ladders of peacocks' tails. Children are natural multipliers' (chapter 5). 'You will ask how one can do so much for so many.

The New Testament As Personal Reading

We are all Adams, one human condition. All clay men, exiles from Eden. God put his hand on Christ's hand to draw the bolt on the gate. It's as if God had played a trick, not a sly trick, but like those that charm children at festival time. He wanted to find himself in us. He sent Christ and it happened' (chapter 5).

'The gamblers come forward at this point. "We now have endless credit with God, so let's go wild and do what we like. Any cheques we draw on evil accounts will bounce." The suggestion is inhuman and absurd. *Noblesse oblige*. Let us suppose your face was clawed to ribbons by a wild animal, and then was restored by a brilliant surgeon, a friend, and the only man on earth, in fact, with the skill to do it. Would you go off looking for another encounter with a wild animal, saying merrily that your friend is always at hand? An extreme example? The extreme is possible only because there is the ordinary. You are extremely tired only because you can be tired to begin with, slightly tired. *Noblesse oblige* holds with friends even if it's only some social solecism that's at stake. You may read me on those lines in *Corinthians*.'

'I'll give you a monstrous example. Suppose, this time, you were married and had ten children, all so gross and deformed that you had to hide them in a cave. They all die, and their mother as well. You marry again and are blessed with many children, brave as David and lovely as Ruth. Apply that to your new life in Christ. Sin is your monstrous and deformed child' (chapters 6-7).

'You are now going to say that you have found me out in a contradiction. I am saying, am I not, that the law is sin? And it is God's law. My answer is, not really, not at all. I shall go autobiographical. As you

The Olive Tree in the Forum

know, a Jewish boy enters the community of worship at thirteen or fourteen. The law is then presented to him formally, the law and its obligations.'

'You also know from experience that that age is the beginning of the painful process towards maturity; a painful, turbulent and rebellious phase. I say, do I not, that I should never have known what covetousness was unless the law said, "You shall not covet." That's too bald, too oversimplified. What I mean is that I was mature enough to know I now had the burden of what that law entails. And I discovered the gap between the real and the ideal. That's a Greek way of speaking, not properly, if I were Plato, but it makes the point.'

'Overscrupulous, you may say. So be it. A man, or a boy, has to live with his own agony, the acuteness varies. I was, until Christ found me, an intense perfectionist, a law-man bristling with jots and tittles, dotting the i's and crossing the t's of obligations *ad infinitum*. But I failed. I was a prisoner of failure and a prisoner of the absolute demands of the law in one and the same prison. Who was to rescue me? That perpetual quirk in human nature bit deeply. You know it. Forbidden fruit is sweetest.'

'The law has a granite force, so abstract and impersonal. I was, I expect, unconsciously looking for someone who would show me how God really saw me, and you, and all mankind.'

'I grant that the law is good. Its essential drive is God-given and noble, but it broke my heart. The law has grown sclerotic through abnormal growths, man-made and inhuman. Man always tends to imprison other men even with religious shackles. That's what happened to the law: too much of the officialdom of our fallen nature in charge of the official edition, mandatory for Jews.'

The New Testament As Personal Reading

'I re-act too much, but for good reason. In less strained moments I would have to admit I knew many noble Pharisees, and there are historical reasons too for the law's disease. Not all the calcifers were hypocrites. Much is due to the siege mentality of my beleagured people, many of whom have a dour sincerity. It is hard for anyone to question tradition. There were, of course, as always the ugly facets — the corpulent piety of the careerist marching through the *agora* at the head of a brass and cymbals band.'

'Christ came on earth, flesh like me, born of woman. He lived the human life and did not falter. If you look at Christ's life, and witnesses are still alive and writing preliminary sketches, you know he was, humanly speaking, all God could want of man: the high points of Deuteronomy and the Prophets verified in him in an incredible manifestation of love and mercy, and mercy is love moved at the sight of misery. You know intuitively this is *IT*. In Christ God was invading the world again in earnest, overpowering your soul and helping you to see, through chinks of faith, that he was re-creating the world.'

'And what happened to Christ? Men could not bear so much love. To be very charitable, it was most embarrassing for the vested interests, the smiling professionals, the politicians and the establishment theologians. So they edged him on to the cross, with a not unreasonable show, from their point of view, of legal expedients. Ordinary Jews, the people of the land, were not consulted. In that, Christ too was an ordinary Jew. He died without a referendum.'

'The cross, the universal nail plunged into eternal love, was consumed by fire from heaven. When the conflagration was well over, I speak very clumsily, I saw Christ alive, in heaven and on earth, on the road

The Olive Tree in the Forum

to Damascus. Love and death can never *finally* co-exist. That's why I call sin death or death sin. "O death where is thy victory," I said to the Corinthians. It fits even better here.'

'Looking back now, I must have seen a gleam of it all in those Christians I persecuted when I was super-lawman. All put together, I now call the life of the Spirit. The Lord should have a middle name, Jesus *Genesis* Christ. His blood moved over the face of the waters. What a divine re-writing of the dictum of Archimedes! "Give me a place to be crucified and I shall move the universe" ' (chapters 7-8).

'We are still pilgrims, but the best is yet to be. We still share the pangs of creation. People hunger, people have diseases, people fight, people die. Listen. We are massive in hope. We are possessed by God in Christ, and nothing can take that away' (chapter 8).

'I am now anti-semitic? God forbid. Look at the Jewish past. It's still alive. God's promises to Israel, the sonship, the law, the covenants. Christ is a Jew. Face and hands and feet. It breaks my heart. I'd cease to be a Christian if that would bring my people to Christ. There is only one bouquet fit for the tomb of the patriarchs, lilies of the field from Carmel placed there by Christ.'

'You must have noticed there have always been two roads in Jewish history, and one not taken. You had an Isaac, but what about the other sons? You had a Jacob, but what about the brothers? That's God's secret. Besides, God never confined himself to the Jews exclusively.'

'But, the promises, the promises! Let me go to an image. Israel is still God's olive tree. It has lost the Jewish branches but other branches have been grafted on — Greek, Roman, and barbarian branches.

The New Testament As Personal Reading

But God holds the fallen branches in reserve, and you know that in God's day you can see forever. I know he is looking ahead, and one day will restore the fallen branches on a universal olive tree. In a mysterious way the fallen branches are still part of the growth and God is not a gardener like Adam' (chapters 9-11).

'Where do we stand after all that long digression? First of all, we have our obligations to remember. We must shorten the distance between man and man by love. We must be responsible citizens. Pay our debts. Be earnest. Among Christians it is always the pre-dawn of eternity.'

'Now, some tiresome details. You fight about the sabbath and questions of diet. These are not the essential. Honour the other man's motives. You are both God's.'

'Be discreet. Don't do the big liberal thing, even when you are right, if that upsets a decent man who does not have *your* intelligence, or your powers of perception. Christ did not please himself. A mother walks at the pace of the slowest child, loving all her children equally' (chapters 14-15).

'I'll call on you on my way to Spain. Be kind to Phoebe when she reaches Rome. Greet all my friends. A word to Rufus. I regard his mother as mine too. My secretary, Tertius, will add his own P.S. to the glory of God.'

So far, *Romans* in paraphrase and all the perils of modernizing Paul, made by a lapsed scholar and *diplochronoglot*, which is someone who tries, using a two-way system, to make 70 A.D. and 1981 A.D. swap thoughts and language, and not betray the mind and heart of Paul.

If an earnest and intelligent youth were to say: 'I find the granite ramparts of *Romans* daunting', this

The Olive Tree in the Forum

is what the *diplochronoglot* would say to him.

'There is a very old Englishman you should go to see. His father was Jewish, his mother Italian. As a very young man he was terribly wounded as a subaltern with the Munster Fusiliers in Gallipoli, 1915. He is a widower and most eccentric. He goes to Mass every day, is bitterly opposed to euthanasia and abortion, tries to grow grapes in window-boxes in Kent and was a breeder of champion bulldogs.'

'Once he knew his St Paul very well indeed, but now he has reached the stage when the interior narrative that holds him together is really a peaceful mixture. He never knows whether he is quoting St Paul, life's exegesis on himself, or his general culture. His name is Peter Wanderwide, a man of the larger air.'

'What he will say to you is this.

Keep walking around those granite ramparts, and before you are my age, or maybe not until then, you will find a gate, abandoned by the sentries, a flaming sword and the cherubim, since 33 A.D.

If you believe, and look in, since you may not enter until you die, you will see, as in a glass darkly, but you will see, a garden. From time to time you will see it in great clarity and people in it.

Dante, for instance, speaking to Beatrice by a bridge on the river of Eden, which no longer divides. And you will hear him say to her as you might hear the sound of surf from a very distant Dover Beach, "In your eyes I saw Christ."

And you will see Saladin, no longer alone, and you will hear him say, like the sound of springs, but very close, where the Jordan gathers itself near Caesarea Philippi, "I never thought Christ could remake so many."

And Christ and Paul in the sun among the ol-

The New Testament As Personal Reading

ives. Christ's face you will not see, yet, and there will be no sound of any kind to be heard except Paul's voice. That will be very clear, and much closer than the sounds you heard before. "Lord, Dante told me what he said about your Father, but I have changed it a little for you." "You are the love on earth that moves mankind, the sun and the other stars." '

For Yours is the Kingdom . . .
— The Beatitudes

Thomas Waldron

It is hard to imagine Christ being satisfied with a draw. He must sometimes settle for it and sometimes accept defeat but he is committed to victory, not partial victory but total victory, not immediate victory but final victory. The religion which we call by his name, it too has a Kerry, a Liverpool, a Welsh quality — a disbelief in ultimate defeat or limited achievement. The Kingdom will come.

I do not flippantly use the language of sport to express mysteries. Paul is my distant ancestor and it is remarkable how much the language of people's popular interests — the language of where their hearts and purest commitments are — is the language of salvation. The sports pages reflect metaphorically the final reality of struggle, the cardinal virtues of belief, confidence and support, the possibility of losing, and victory and celebration.

They reflect too mankind's desire for complete victory — the popular *Weltanschauung*, the World Cup, the World Series, the World Championship. This again is the dimmed reflection of Christ's world concern. For God's story begins with the whole world and the all-mankind of Eden; Christ comes as the light which is to enlighten every man and his disciples are given a mission to all nations. The chalice of suffering will become the cup of victory which we shall finally sup from, when the tens and tens of thousands gather

Thomas Waldron is a priest of the Archdiocese of Tuam. He is President of St. Jarlath's College, Tuam, Co. Galway.

The New Testament As Personal Reading

at the Supper of the Lamb.

So often the people — the crowd, that big flock of sheep which Jesus pitied, that clutch of ungathered chickens — unconsciously foreshadow destiny and the divine plan. This is not remarkable because the kingdom that is to come is not only God's but theirs. It is the kingdom they long for, dream of, pray for, a kingdom of justice, love and peace, a kingdom beyond the wear and tear of this life.

And it is their kingdom. It is not a kingdom of small groups but for all. The invitation and mission of Christ is to everybody. Christianity's small groups were never just for group therapy or for the sake of the group, but for the benefit of all. Carmelite nun or Trappist monk are mine and all for me. The Church has always with sure instinct suspected groups which denied salvation to the common people. The light is for everyman. Christ died for the people who read the sports pages, the people of the eighth station, the people he fed — the sandwiches people.

That's one reason why I find it hard to accept that the Beatitudes were addressed to the Disciples only — which is one of the theories about them. Christ was concerned with the mass market. Even if he went after the one sheep he was still shepherd of a hundred — and had other sheep too. And Pope John Paul wondering about his visit to the people of Brazil reached for the Beatitudes: 'When I thought of the way in which I should present myself to the inhabitants of Brazil, I felt the duty of presenting above all the teachings of the eight beatitudes'. Like master, like man.

Of course the Pope is talking about content, but the very cut of the Beatitudes is for the people, the ready-to-wear market. They have the ring of the proverb about them and mankind dearly loves its proverbs.

For Yours is the Kingdom . . .

We seem to like our wisdom in metre and in short — the iambic is the beat of the heart. The truths we do grasp we like them enshrined and accessible.

So I prefer the theory that Christ like the Jewish rabbis of his time — and like good teachers of all times — summarised his teaching and put it in a way that wooed and gratified the ear and the memory. The Beatitudes were a sort of mental phylactery designed to wear well.

The rabbis liked to provide Catechisms and that was where I first met the Beatitudes — in a little book popular in National School, *Catechism Notes*. There were eight of them, and the Seven Dolours, and the Twelve Fruits of the Holy Spirit. They were for grown men of ten and eleven, and we learned them as the man who composed them meant them to be learned — by repetition and by heart. They were made for that — all beginning with the word 'Blessed', all in two parts, the first and last in the present tense and promising the Kingdom of Heaven, the intermediate six in the future — two 'ises' and six 'shalls'. It is nice to think that after 2000 years the same tool of learning had not lost its edge. It's the old pleasure and strength of the formula. It's in Homer, Virgil, Beowulf, the *Fiannaioct*. Humanity has always used it for its epics and the Beatitudes are the story of man's journey to God — of man's lost obedience and the fruit of that forbidden tree — the Cross.

Later I came to preach the Beatitudes, making a sermon of the Sermon, fleshing them out as they flesh out the two great commandments. The Beatitudes need this, for each of them is like a closed concertina, fold and fold compressed but ready to open into long rich meaning. Yet one was conscious as one did it of the pejorative phrase 'preacher's use of scripture'.

The New Testament As Personal Reading

That used to be said by scholars who dealt faithfully with the written bones and who mildly despised fanciful flesh on the skeletal frame. It was a time when the flesh was despised.

But then T.S. Eliot especially made it respectable to say that there was more in poetry than its writer knew, that it bore meanings that awaited discovery. And Biblical scholarship began to say that there was an oral Gospel before there was a written one and that the scripture was anyway simply a summary of what Christ had preached. So the scholar had his place and restored original grace to the preacher, and the preacher realised that he did not need the support of marching Teutonic footnotes to justify every meaning that the Word of God yielded to meditation or imagination.

The Beatitudes are the essential Good News but I remember them as frightening. I read them first as threat not promise. For me they were conditional sentences, 'If you are not pure in heart you shall not see God'. Religion is not obviously Good News, especially not to the young. The little girl who told me she spoke to God often — she used to say 'Shut up, You' — may have many who understand her and would say the same — if they dared. The opposite to the Good News can be very Bad News indeed — outcast, pain, punishment, loss, damned. We can seem to be caught in a game in which we never asked to play and in which the punishment for losing is so terrible that it vitiates all hope and joy in winning. Religion then becomes a set of precautionary measures and Heaven only an escape — the mere absence of Hell.

PROMISES NOT THREATS

My change to seeing the Beatitudes as promises, not

For Yours is the Kingdom . . .

threats, was a function not so much of Vatican II but of aging. Aging is often both wisdom and grace. Youth is a time of hope and promise in most areas but in the spiritual area it is often a time of threat. Perhaps it has (or had — I may be simply reflecting an era) to do with a time when one is so clearly under authority and when the person is under attack from a confusion of feelings. The voice of the merciful Christ, of the wise and comprehending and compassionate Lord is not the *cantus firmus* of adolescence. For youth the serious God is restraining and sometimes minatory. There is at least the suspicion of a thunderbolt up his sleeve.

Strangely, a little later, when the rosy turns to speckled and mottled, the theology of fear yields to a theology of hope and possibility. As you realise in yourself the need for a salvation and what that salvation must mean in personal terms, at that moment you realise that this is what Christ is promising. How could God have come upon the earth to increase our fears, to underline impossibility or to preach an elitist salvation? Anxiety and hopelessness and exclusivity we manufacture at home, we need no visiting God for these. Christ could not have come, seen, helped, and loved people and then bowed out of their lives saying, 'Ah God help them'.

There is only one News that is Good, and that is the word that all the good that is in us, as dream or desire or possibility, will yet come into being. We are trapped, oppressed, powerless but aware and offering, and we need to be. The good is in us, which we can do, which we can be — this must not die; it demands life. We are not destined to be unfinished stories. We need a saviour. We need a kingdom. We cry for completion.

The New Testament As Personal Reading

The Beatitudes are God's answer to the cry he implanted in us, God's catalogue of possible completions. Salvation is available, and is happening at this moment and to us. The Beatitudes introduce a note of sober and exultant and sustaining reality into what was once dream or nightmare. They are promise but current reality too — the pilgrim Church has part of its journey over, the people of God are already future. Hell is a fading fire for 'a royal race and a princely people'.

And the terms of the Beatitudes are concrete and basic, strong truth and assured — we shall see, we shall possess, we shall have, we shall obtain, be filled, be comforted, be called the children of God, and the Kingdom will be ours. There is nothing hazy or visionary or doubtful. We have here the strict promise of God, this is covenant on the edge of final fulfilment.

And this will happen not for vaguely defined, shadowy wraiths but for people with strong hard profiles, people we know, people we can be, people we are — merciful people, gentle people, people whose passion is justice, people whose passion is peace, honest and decent people, people upset by the iniquities and inequities of their world, poor people, suffering people, weak people. The Beatitudes are the ultimate charter of Everyman. They are the measured statements of God, cost calculated, term set, delivery secured on date due. They are hard statements — they are not metaphors to crumble under pressure. Each is like a rock.

THE BEATITUDES AND THE TEMPTATIONS

It may be by accident or design that Matthew sets the Beatitudes almost immediately after the Temptations in his narrative. Nowhere is the difference between

For Yours is the Kingdom . . .

the kingdom of this world and the kingdom that is to come so pointed. The Beatitudes read like Christ's direct rebuttal of the gospel according to Satan. Satan offers things and instant rewards. Oddly enough or not — what he offers is remarkably close to what J.K. Galbraith in *The Affluent Society* names as the functions of wealth — power, prestige and possession — the satisfied appetite, the magical power and name, dominion. These are Satan's miracles. Christ even in his miracles proclaims a different vision — he brings life from death, sight from blindness, movement from immobility, healing from sickness. The Beatitudes are about people raised to new life, the Temptations are about how to succeed in business.

Satan must have been a puzzled angel as he left Christ. His suspicions were confirmed as to who Christ was but he is even less sure what that means. C. S. Lewis once said that a lower order of being cannot conceive how a higher order of being sees, judges, acts — because the higher inhabits a country, breathes an air, has a vision, lives a life of which the lower being has no experience. Satan's offers to Christ are instinct with Satan's misconceptions of what God or goodness is like. Christ's values are without meaning for Satan. Satan can see for the human being no hunger that is not of the belly kind, no power that is not physical, no possessions that are not tangible. For Satan man is a creature of the present, for Christ we are people of the future.

So Satan's promise is instant in its satisfaction. But it bears the marks of its paternity — it is for personal aggrandisement, it is given on condition that you sell yourself and, like many of our special offers, it is 'for a limited time only.' The blessedness of the Beatitudes is by contrast total and forever. It is the fulfilment of

The New Testament As Personal Reading

Boetius's classical definition of happiness. There is no fear of loss. Christ's giving is beyond the power of time or temporalities. His giving is the new and everlasting covenant. In *Hosea* God had said: 'I will take back my corn and my wine . . . I will retrieve my wool, my flax'. But now with Christ there is no taking back. The gifts of the Beatitudes are complete and absolute. It is the fulfilment of the promise made later in *Hosea:*

> I will betroth you to myself forever,
> With integrity and justice,
> With tenderness and love,
> With faithfulness,
> And you will come to know Yahweh.
> I will sow him in the country,
> I will love Unloved;
> I will say to No-People-of-Mine,
>   'You are my people';
> And he will answer, 'You are my God'.

The final gift is being, citizenship in the kingdom of heaven. Satan's gifts are commerce and they are accretions — bits added on to the person. Christ's are covenant and they are integral.

Even specifically the Beatitudes reject the world system of the Temptations. The hunger which deeply matters is the hunger for righteousness — and part of that is the hunger to see that the hungry are fed not as a bribe but as a matter of right. The earth will indeed be given, but to the gentle — they who watched the rats race will receive what the rats raced for, because they will respect and do no violence to the earth. A kingdom will be received but it is the kingdom of heaven and its recipients will be the poor and the suffering. The power of God will be used — not for catching the mountebank but for the comforting of those

For Yours is the Kingdom . . .

saddened by the evil of the world, and for the reward of those who tried to make peace. And heaven is won not bought, it is a matter of being not having. Christ in the Beatitudes rejects the instant acquisition that Satan offered. In the divine economy, in God's usual way there is no totally unearned income. In Bonhoeffer's phrase there is no such thing as cheap grace. Discipleship is costly. Heaven is not as easy as falling off a log — or jumping off a pinnacle. Heaven is goodness slow-ripening into sanctity. Heaven is long suffering crowned with peace. Heaven is earnest prayer become lasting achievement. Heaven is hunger finally satisfied at the Supper of the Lamb. Heaven is the home of which all other homes were pale images — the place that our hearts have spent a lifetime beating for, hoping for, believing in

> My people will live in a peaceful home,
> In safe houses,
> In quiet dwellings.
>
> (Is. 32 18).

THE BLESSED IN HEAVEN

The Beatitudes are really the demography of Heaven, its population by categories, a census of the saints. Who are the Blessed? These are the Blessed. They inhabit the many mansions that make up his Father's house, but they are all at home. These are Christ's own who in one way or other have confessed him before men, who bear one mark or other of the Crucified — his poverty, his pain, his mercy, his hunger, his gentleness, his peace, his generosity. These are God's people at journey's end.

But they're not weary pilgrims. These are the victorious at home. Imagine them in a room together.

The New Testament As Personal Reading

The assurance and approbation of victory invests each of them. They are confirmed in joy. As in every victory there is only delicious unity and gratitude. They are more perfectly what they were in life — now all for others with no trace whatever of selfishness or competition or jealousy.

It would be a gathering of total generosity. To their delight they would find here in each other the people they championed on earth. The final comfort of the mourners is to find here the poor for whom they mourned. Those who thirsted for justice are ecstatic to meet here, and happy the gentle and downtrodden whose liberation they hungered for. And the persecuted will at last meet the merciful. Heaven is like that, if we can believe the Beatitudes — not just us with our goodness but those our goodness was for. We save each other.

In that room there could be surprise too. The people of the Beatitudes as Christ portrays them are quite different in character. When they meet they will find present some who, they thought, were opposed to them on earth. Quite obviously those who hunger and thirst after justice often have little patience with the peacemakers or the meek or the merciful. Here on earth, too, there are people with the same hunger and the same vision who travel by different roads and directions, and who mistake one another for enemies. They take opposite ways of reaching the same goal, or they travel the same road walled off from one another by colour or creed or nationality or ideology. People who are passionate in their differences and perhaps saw themselves as irreconcilable will find that their God is well pleased with both his children and they will share the same reward. They will be delighted to find they are brothers and regret only — if there can

For Yours is the Kingdom . . .

be regret in heaven — that they did not come to know each other sooner. God will reward their honesty and their passion as it dawns fully on them in his light and that their real achievement is not on earth but in heaven.

'Theirs is the Kingdom of Heaven' — the promise of the First Beatitude and the last. It is not, I think, accidental that the Beatitudes open and close with the promise of the kingdom. The kingdom is the all-embracing concept. Indeed Christ's last public statement of his mission is, 'I am a king but mine is not a kingdom of this world'. In that kingdom are his gathered people, the immortal wheat of Traherne harvested. In the Beatitudes they reflect each other's goodness, in the Kingdom they reflect and mirror each other's glory. The first and last Beatitudes suggest the enveloping grace of the Kingdom where light is added to light, to light, to light — the immortal diamond of Hopkins in its final setting, the many-faceted Christ.

CHRIST, FIRST OF THE BLESSED

For Christ is there too, the pleased Teacher of the Sermon with successful pupils — but much more than that. Here is the vine and its branches, here is the Mystical Body and its members, here Christ is with his friends. They are each the embodiment of part of his goodness and he is the embodiment of all their goodness. For Christ is not just the teacher of the Beatitudes but their exemplar and first model.

On the cross Christ exemplifies the first part of each Beatitude. He is the poor — who was without power and had nowhere to lay his head. He is the gentle who broke no bruised reed. He has mourned over Jerusalem and longed to gather his people to him. He hangs

The New Testament As Personal Reading

between heaven and earth because he has hungered and thirsted for what is right. He is merciful even as he dies. He is the pure in heart who set his face towards Jerusalem and accepted the chalice of his father's will. He came with the promise of peace and peace was his greeting. He is the persecuted one, the Suffering Servant, 'for our faults struck down in death' (Is. 53:8). Suddenly the good thief recognised him and knew that his was the kingdom.

Christ rose to inherit that kingdom. All the Beatitudes find their most complete fulfilment in the Risen Christ. If no other proof were present of the reality of Christ's resurrection and divinity, the difference between the one like us who was in agony and the one who now appears calm in the power and certain identity of God might well suffice. Christ risen is divinely assured but now separate from the human condition 'his soul's anguish over'. He is one with the Father and fully the Son of God in his own being. He has entered into possession of the kingdom prepared for him. The earth is his and the times and the ages.

Our fulfilment, since we have been baptised into his death, will be like Christ's. The prophecy 'ye shall be like gods' — the destiny of man in Eden — culminates in the Blessed. Christ is all those Blessed people, the summation of the Beatitudes. We, of course, are partial people pursuing our limited and limiting vocations. We have the aspirations to do everything but the realisation that we are circumscribed by time and energy and ability and a host of other limitations. Sometimes too, despite the aspiration, we sin, we go, as God said, into 'exile for want of perception'. Most of us are smallholders tilling a patch of ground. But the aspiration is our window looking on to the immense possibility that Baptism and Eucharist and Passion

For Yours is the Kingdom . . .

and Resurrection prepare us for. We plod to point Omega but we are more conscious of the plodding than Christ is. For him we are the Blessed he spoke of, following where he has led.

The Christian is future governed. Christ the exemplar of the Beatitudes is the exemplar of our destiny. For each of us who lives in some way the first part of some Beatitude he is in Rilke's words, 'the coming one, imminent from all eternity, the future one, the final fruit of a tree whose leaves we are'.

We are easily aware and persuaded of this in the case of the saints — those we read about, those we know. They are obviously Beatitude people marked by the signs of faith. These are the people Austen Farrar writes of: 'Men whose words are like their faces, and their faces like their hearts and theirs hearts printed with the cross of Christ.'

These are the champions. But the Beatitudes are about the many, the ordinary. They're about the people you'd like to see in Heaven, I'd like to see in Heaven. And if we can see the goodness which we should love to preserve, perfect, and enjoy forever, I think Christ will be no less aware than we.

I want to see there the young plumber who refused the extra wage I offered and asked me to give it to Trocaire. Blessed are the merciful . . .

I want to see the girl who refused the £10,000 a year job in favour of her friend who had seen the advertisement first. Blessed are the clean of heart . . .

I want to see the old alcoholic priest of whom a man said to me, 'He's so good that when I get to heaven I'll have a crick in my neck looking up at him'. Blessed are the gentle . . .

And I do not think that Christ exhausted the Beat-i-tudes when he named only eight. So I want to see

The New Testament As Personal Reading

Tom for his sense of humour, Dick for his kindness, Harry for his patience.

There are all sorts and conditions of people who must be there. There will be Christians and non-Christians. The Christians perhaps offer their goodness more consciously for they are privileged in Joan Didion's phrase to be 'the elected representatives of the invisible city'. The non-Christians are those Christ was equally aware of, those not of this fold. All the goodness there is, all the pain there is — small decencies, small mercies, great loves, great sorrows — he takes and marks for salvation. He exalts all our virtues into passports to his kingdom. All people are his people for Christ came to save the world.

So the *denouement* of the Beatitudes is the Wedding Feast of the Lamb. It is to this that they point and lead. The throngs who will sit down at the feast are the people nominated by Christ in Galilee. In the Beatitudes Christ displayed so many wedding garments for our wearing. Each guest wears now and forever a garment woven in time. The bride wears the dazzling white linen which 'is made of the good deeds of the saints'. The angel proclaims the final Beatitude: 'Happy are those who are invited to the Wedding Feast of the Lamb'. The Blessed enter their kingdom. It is *eschaton* and *pleroma*, the fullness of time. The lone voice which in Palestine said, 'Blessed are the . . .' is answered by 'the voices of a huge crowd like the sound of the ocean or a great roar of thunder, crying: 'Alleluia, The reign of the Lord, Our God Almighty has begun'.

Great Deeds in Young Churches
— the Acts of the Apostles

Donal Dorr

Last year was difficult, a long grind. A time when I often had to turn for nourishment and fortitude to tales of heroes. A few pages were enough to carry me into some story of courage, endurance and salvation. It didn't matter too much whether the characters were Greeks of two thousand years ago, or Tolkien's hobbits, or even the rabbits of *Watership Down;* for any of the stories could provide a glimpse of the one salvation story, the risk and gift of seeking and finding how to become human in an inhuman world. I was surprised to find (though I should not have been) that *The Acts of the Apostles* provides the same kind of inspiration. These 'acts' have a certain heroic quality. In Irish they could be called *'gaisci'* — like the adventures of Cuchulann or St Brendan, or like the 'famous deeds' of the Playboy of the Western World. But there's nothing unreal about the great deeds of *Acts*. This is an everyday kind of heroism, the kind that calls me to follow the same path. Which is why it nourishes my spirit when the road ahead is dark and tiring.

It is not surprising then that the author of *Acts* inserted those famous 'we' passages. He wanted to show that the story was not just about 'them' but was about himself also. And the book of the *Acts* remains open-ended in a way. I can add a chapter or two my-

---

Donal Dorr is a priest of St Patrick's Missionary Society, Kiltegan, Co. Wicklow. At present holder of the Cardinal Conway Research Fellowship in the Theology of Development at St Patrick's College, Maynooth.

The New Testament As Personal Reading

self and so can you. If we do it together we are Church, writing our own 'we' passages.

ACTS OF APOSTLES, ACTS OF GOD

In many ways, *Acts* is more the story of great events than of great deeds. The heroes are being acted upon more than acting; think of Pentecost (2:1-4), Saul's conversion (9:3-8), Peter's vision of the unclean food (10:9-16), the escapes from prison (12:6-10; 16:25-26) and so on. Behind the great acts of the apostles lie the great acts of God. And that's really the whole point of the story. That's what gives unity to a rag-bag of tales about Peter and Paul, along with the supporting cast of Stephen, James, Mark, Barnabas etc. The overall message is: Something great has been going on here; behind all the ups and downs — the arrests and escapes, the stoning and shipwreck, the healing and plotting, the warm welcomes and the angry rejections — through and beyond them all there's a pattern.

The Good News *is* the pattern. It is not something added on from outside but is the reality of what has been going on — its real meaning recognized by faith. Faith fits the various items into a pattern: the death of Stephen and James are as much a victory as the rescue of Peter and of Paul. All kinds of events are understood to be from the hand of God, part of the story of salvation, the Good News: Philip's hitch-hike on the road to Gaza (8:26-39), a riot in Ephesus (19:28-41), even a difference of opinion between Paul and Barnabas (15:39). So faith is not something out of this world. It is the gift of being able to see what is really happening in daily life. The ability to see each event and action of life as a *'gaisce'*, a might deed. Our little deeds of courage and endurance, of celebration and disputation, our little victories and defeats — even the

Great Deeds in Young Churches

final defeat of death — all these are the stuff of the mighty deeds of God.

It is easy to see that *Acts* comes from the same hand as the Emmaus story (Luke 24:13-33). On the road to Emmaus, Jesus showed the disciples what had really been happening from the time of Moses right up to the life and death of Jesus himself. This 'inside story' left their hearts burning within them. In *Acts* we have Emmaus, Part Two. It is designed to leave *our* hearts burning within us, as we recognize how the history of salvation has continued in the daily life of the young Church. But the whole purpose of the Emmaus story and the *Acts* will have been missed if you and I fail to move on to Emmaus, Part Three — the story of the hand of God in the pattern of history, in the life of the world and especially of the Christian community, right down to the events of your life and mine.

In the transition from the Gospels to our lives, the *Acts* has a crucially important role. It is easy to put Christ's preaching and healing and life-style in a special-category zone where its relevance to our living is not fully appreciated. But who could deny that Dorcas (9:36) and Ananias (5:1) and Stephen (6:8) — and even Peter and Paul — had experiences very like ours? If stories about what they did are part of the story of salvation then I'm encouraged to try and see my actions and yours as part of salvation history also. That's what faith means. Maybe it is no accident that *Acts* doesn't have a rounded ending. The writer stopped there but the 'acts' go on. There's continuity between the acts of Jesus, the *Acts* of the apostles, and our acts today.

UNIVERSAL MISSION

Acts is thought of as the missionary book of the Bible.

The New Testament As Personal Reading

It would be a pity if this were understood only in the superficial sense that it recounts Paul's missionary journeys. For the crucial missionary elements of *Acts* come long before Paul takes to the road. There is first of all the source of the missionary impulse of the Church. This is the Pentecost experience. To be a Christian one must share in it; and when one shares in it one feels impelled to share it with others. It is the sense of being touched by the power of God in a way that gives hope, courage and vision. It is an experience that renews the old and the frightened so that they can dream of a new future and set out to realize it (2:14-17).

A second stage is when it dawns on the young Church that the vision is truly universal, that it is open to all cultures. Not merely open to all who are willing to adopt Jewish customs but also to those who want to be Christian while retaining their own cultures. Of course Paul played a crucial role in helping the young Church to accept this universality. But the crucial experience was that of Peter. His vision of the unclean food (10:9-16) prepared him to 'see clearly that the Jews are not God's only favourites' (10:34 *Living Bible* paraphrase).

A good deal of the central part of the *Acts* is the account of the exciting and painful working out in practice of the implications of this basic insight. The Council of Jerusalem (15:5-30) is the high point, a model against which we in the Church today may fruitfully measure ourselves. Are we putting God to the test by burdening people (and peoples) with excessive burdens (as Peter asked) (15:10)? Are we inclined to confuse bits of our cultural and legal heritage with the essentials of Christian faith? (cf. 15:28). Equally important: how do we set out to find answers to these awkward questions? Do we only rely on our past tradition? The apostles took account of tradition; but they also gave space to Barnabas and Paul to share their recent experiences (15:12). They listened to the account of how God was found to be working in unexpected ways, among unlikely people. And James, the champion of the conservatives, took the risk of welcoming the new manifestation of Good News — and of finding a formula that reconciled the two groups (15:13-21).

So *Acts* inspires us to 'discern the signs of the times' — to be willing to look for the action of God far beyond the boundaries we have set up and within which we expect to find him at work. But, conversely, it also encourages us to look in unexpected places for an entry-point for the insertion of the story of Jesus. What strikes me most vividly about the style of Paul as a missionary is the variety and flexibility of his approach. We have something to learn both from the way he worked in Corinth and from the very different approach he adopted in Athens. In Corinth he spent years sharing the life and work of the ordinary working people there. It really challenges me to find that a man with the burning sense of mission that Paul had, a man called to be 'a chosen instrument' to carry the Lord's name before Gentiles and Jews (9:15) — to find that he thinks it worthwhile to 'waste' time making tents (18:3). Not merely a 'worker priest' but a 'worker bishop'! Is this saying something to us today about the importance of ministers being in solidarity with working people?

In Athens, Paul got his entry point by finding some of the deep hopes and fears of people, expressed in their homage to 'the Unknown God' (17:23). He was able to attune himself to these deep but obscure hearers rather than merely talking *at* them. And he seemed to be prepared to work with the few who really responded rather than worrying about getting through to a mass audience.

The missionary approach of Paul in Athens raises questions about our approach today both at home and in the Third World. We may be so concerned about the content of our message, our *answers*, that we don't give a high priority to discovering and resonating with the questions that people are actually asking and the concerns they have. For instance, I found in Africa that for many people the basic question about God is not, 'how many persons are there in the Trinity?' or even, 'how many Gods are there, if any?' rather the big issue is, 'can God really cope with the problems of evil that affect me?' So at least part of my preaching has to be not just about 'the Unknown God', or the loving God, but about the powerful God.

Those who work on the home mission may too easily assume that they are already in touch with the deep concerns and fears of the people among whom they work. There may be barriers and insensitivity, failures to be in real solidarity with the local people. The ministers may come from a different social class, or be educated into a different class. This applies most obviously in those urban areas where manual workers or the jobless live; but it can also apply in rural areas. And where preachers experience real solidarity with some of their people, it is frequently with one social class. Maybe we need some more tent-making ministers, preachers who share the lives of different kinds of workers.

TRUST IN THE SPIRIT

At times it can be very refreshing for me to work 'on

Great Deeds in Young Churches

the missions', in the Young Churches. Some of what goes on could fit quite comfortably into the *Acts*. For instance, the missionary may find himself/herself doing what Paul and Barnabas did along the riverbank in Philippi (16:13-15) — just making contacts, accepting hospitality, and helping to build up a community from there. But sadly, the old and new Churches today have far more in common with each other than the young Churches of the Third World have in common with the young Churches of *Acts*. We seem to be operating the same inflexible model of Church all over the world, having abandoned the flexibility and inventiveness and sheer trust that permeates the *Acts*. For example, I recently heard an Irish bishop speak to parish leaders on the text of *Acts* 6:2-4 about the appointment of the seven deacons. He spoke eloquently, and many of his audience were touched by his words. But he didn't advert at all to one significant phrase in the text: 'Choose seven men . . .' — it was the community rather than the apostles who were to do the choosing. It struck me how rarely the successors of the apostles ask the community to choose their own leaders or ministers. Just as I was inclined to become judgemental about this, I recalled that when I was working with parish leaders in Africa I too found it easier — and safer — for me to do the choosing.

But the *Acts* doesn't really encourage one to play safe, but rather to take risks in faith and in trust. This applies especially in regard to the question of getting 'dug in' to a place. The life of Paul was a fascinating mixture of putting down roots and of pulling them up again. He became deeply involved in the life of the local community while he was with them. Yet he seems to have had no qualms about leaving a young Christian community to care for its own needs when the

The New Testament As Personal Reading

Spirit called him to work somewhere else. At home and abroad many ministers have difficulties both in getting rooted and in getting up-rooted. I find myself slow to become fully involved because I feel I shall have to move on before too long. Yet I find it hard to move on because I don't fully trust people to manage without me! Recently I was challenged by a friend in a way that seems to accord with the spirit of the *Acts:* 'Be with us fully while you are here and leave us to worry about how we'll get on when you are gone'.

In this and in all the other tricky questions in *Acts* the answer does not come from some rule-book. It comes from listening to the Spirit. One of the most explicit instances is 16:6-9 where the Spirit prevents Paul from going into Asia and calls him instead into Macedonia. Why do we find it more difficult in the Church today to hear the Spirit? Perhaps we can listen *to* the Spirit only when we commit ourselves to listening *for* the Spirit. In other words we must be not only open but eagerly expectant, actively seeking out the call of God in our surroundings, in the paths that open up before us and in the doors that close in our faces. It is a faith that is not just a set of doctrines but an experience of God's presence in our lives and an active search for his call. The role of the minister is to give the kind of leadership given by Peter in his three addresses in the first three chapters of *Acts:* he helps people recognize how God has been at work and he suggests practical ways of cooperating in that work. This is how people receive 'the good news promised to the fathers' (13:32). And the final test is not some abstract criterion of truth. It is rather the fact that in the long run the power of God is unstoppable, as Gamaliel wisely points out (5:38-9). What we are called to do by the *Acts of the Apostles* is to recognize the winning side — and make sure we are on it.

Set Free for Freedom
— the Letter to the Galatians

Enda McDonagh

It is not that the devil has the best lines but that the best words undergo the worst corruptions. *Corruptio optimi* . . . The case-history of 'love' is notorious. It could happen to any rich and serious word. It has happened endlessly to 'freedom'. The current possibility of the 'freedom-loving' nations of the West and 'peace-loving' nations of the East totally destroying one another and the world, reveals the extensive corruption of two great words. Crimes committed in the name of freedom from Ballykelly to Beirut, Kabul and San Salvador make it increasingly difficult to engage in discussion of freedom or liberation or emancipation without provoking cynicism or apathy. Theologians and the Churches may not readily adopt a holier than this world attitude to the discussion. The fact that freedom is a great Christian and theological as well as human and worldly word cannot obscure the Church's own failures to protect and promote freedom in the course of its history. The Inquisition may be untypical and often unfairly presented. There is a history of 'fear of freedom' as a dominant Church attitude which still recurs today. This is where Paul and the Galatians provide a continuing judgement on and stimulus to our understanding and practice of Christian freedom.

Paul 'riles easy'. A few sentences into his letter to the Galatians (Celts in origin) he is hurling ana-

Enda McDonagh is Professor of Moral Theology at St Patrick's College, Maynooth. His latest book is *The Making of Disciples*.

The New Testament As Personal Reading

themas. Ironically his anathema for 'those who would preach another Gospel', frequently invoked by later 'conservatives', is directed against the conservative 'Judaizers' who wish to impose the demands of Jewish law on Gentile Christians. This is the *casus belli* of the letter. Paul had checked this out at Jerusalem. Later he had to confront Peter about it at Antioch. The law does not apply to the Gentiles. Justification, salvation, liberation is not by law but by faith. It is therefore not a human but a divine achievement by God in Jesus Christ. Set free by Jesus, sharing in the promise of freedom to Abraham and his seed, shall the Galatians now exchange new freedom for old slavery? The reproofs and the arguments, the appeals to scripture and experience, the vision opened up of human freedom and unity, all this comes tumbling from Paul's passionate pen. He had come a sick man to the Galatians with this message of faith and freedom and had been enthusiastically received by them. Now in undoubtedly better health, indeed fighting fit, he must recall them to that original faith and freedom.

BEYOND THE LAW AND THE LAWS

The passion of Paul's rejection of the law and his defence of freedom for the Christian might appear naive to the word-weary, even freedom-weary Christians of today. The sophistication of his theological argument and the realism of his vision of the world ought to dispel the suspicion of *naiveté*. Yet the burden of history, of Church law and practice make us hesitant to share his enthusiasms. Were legal requirements of Judaism that much more extensive and inhibiting than subsequent Church laws? And where have the liberated Christians been all these centuries? Devices of rhetoric perhaps but useful reminders of how much we

Set Free for Freedom

need to recover the Pauline vision of Christians as a people set free and the Pauline passion in upholding that vision.

A people set free from the law certainly, from the trivial requirements of a fussy Church bureaucracy which never quite disappears. The days when a hatless priest in Galway was taken to be a Tuam priest have gone. Clerical presence in the wings at the Abbey seems scarcely credible today. These were the *trivia*. No doubt others persist and new ones emerge. Paul's critical view of his apostolic colleagues in surrendering to Jewish legalism provides a permanent basis for scrutinizing Church laws and regulations, their number and detail.

Multiplicity and triviality of law, for all their erosion of Christian freedom, were not Paul's prime target. That was the status of law as way of achieving salvation. By observance of law people aspired to justify themselves in the sight of God, to save themselves. (Echoes here of the Pharisee and the Publican.) This of course is 'another Gospel' (1:7). Faith not law is the way of justification (2:16, *passim*). The achievement is divine not human. In Jesus Christ, the promise made to Abraham and his seed is fulfilled (3:6 ff.). The faith of Abraham anticipated Christian faith in accepting God's initiative and achievement. The complex arguments about Abraham's seed as singular (Jesus Christ) and his true posterity (the Christians) as children of the free woman, Sarah (3:16 f.; 9:21-31) reinforce (and obscure) basic Pauline themes, developed more fully, for example, in his letter to the Romans. Justification, salvation is the free gift of God. Faith is the human way of acceptance. By that acceptance Christians are set free from the law and the other traditional slaveries of sin and of death (Romans).

The New Testament As Personal Reading

The evangelical questions remain strange to Catholic ears; Are you saved? Have you been born again? Have you received the Spirit? Yet they reflect something of the thrust of Paul's concerns with the primacy and totality of the divine achievement in addressing the Galatians. The terminology of freedom, more akin to Paul's usage and thought here, tends to be used in more secular contexts such as the struggle for liberation, the emancipated or liberated woman, the free spirit, the independent mind. For Paul the divine achievement of human liberation is not confined to religious issues or some condition beyond history and out of this world, as will presently appear. The 'liberationists' and 'independents' capture an essential aspect of his message. The temptation to self-justification by observance of the law continues to trouble Christians and may assume strongly religious trappings. In its extreme forms it may paralyze the scrupulous. In a particularly unattractive form it issues in the self-righteousness of the respectable. In middle-class and clerical life this is our greatest temptation. The self-righteousness may easily slide into power-consciousness, not least because power is usually given to the respectable and so acceptable. However the power transfer occurs, the desire to rule, to regulate, to legislate has affected Christian leaders in ways similar to secular leaders. Despite Jesus' warning not to behave as secular rulers the temptation has frequently proved too much.

FREEDOM IN COMMUNITY

In the spate of regulations and efficiency of administration the freedom of the Christian finds little room for expression and development. There are many Church leaders who see themselves as promoters and

Set Free for Freedom

protectors of authentic Christian freedom. Authentic, as so often, is the catch. Without people and structures to test the authenticity leaders can easily deceive themselves about their commitment to freedom. Paul confronting Peter of Antioch in the name of freedom (2:11) still constitutes an unusual Christian event. The promise of collegiality and co-responsibility throughout the Church which emerged after Vatican II still provides hope of a leadership and collaboration dedicated to the development of a freed and free people, the people of God. The Synod of Bishops, the Pastoral Council of England and Wales, the open collegial style of many bishops' conferences, for example, South African, the development of lay commissioners, the diocesan assemblies of clergy are all indications, however limited, that the free collaboration of a free people can give effective voice to Paul's message of Christian freedom.

The close link between freedom and community in Paul's vision reaches its climax in his famous reversal of the contemporary Jewish prayer in which the male Jew gave thanks that he was born neither Gentile nor slave nor female. For Paul 'there is neither Jew nor Greek, there is neither slave nor free, there is nether male nor female. For you are all one in Christ Jesus' (3:38). Traditional divisions based on race or religion, class or sex are undermined by God's action in Jesus Christ. The barriers must come down. A new kind of community is born. There is a new Israel, even a new Creation. Exodus and Genesis are superseded in the Kingdom inaugurated by Jesus and proclaimed by Paul.

The liberation for all captives which Isaiah promised and Jesus announced (Is. 58:6; 61:1, 2; Lk. 4:16-21) applies to the Galatian Christians of about 50

AD. Attempts to restrict this by the Judaizers move Paul to his denunciation of privileges and barriers and his declaration of 'liberty, equality and fraternity' as characteristic of the new Israel, the new people of God.

The truly radical reform of human relationships accomplished in Jesus has always proved too much for human institutions. Paul was already struggling with this difficulty and sought to clarify it at least for the Galatians. Vatican II in various ways attempted to renew this Pauline vision. In the Constitution on the Church it moved from the Church as mystery of God's presence in the world (a divine not a human achievement) to the Church as people, sharing the radical equality of daughters and sons of the Father and so in chapter three to the service structures. As the secular philosophers and their political disciples discovered much later, liberty, including Christian liberty, emerges and develops in community (fraternity) and involves the mutual respect and acceptance of basic equality.

As the historical sign, embodiment and promoter of God's presence and saving power, of his Kingdom, the Church must realize and give witness to the freedom, equality and unity of human beings in Christ. In the recovered image of Vatican II, repeatedly invoked by Pope John Paul II, the Church is to be the sacrament, the sign and the realization of the community of humankind with its essential accompaniments of freedom and equality. The work of salvation as work of liberation calls the Church to manifest in itself and promote in the world liberty, unity and equality.

Overcoming the divisions and enjoying the freedom were not to be recognized in principle and ignored in practice. And they were not to be relegated to the next

Set Free for Freedom

world. They had to be fought for in this world, in Galatia in 50 AD, in Ireland and a thousand other places in 1983 AD. There was a concrete content affecting the relations between Jew and Gentile, slave and free, man and woman.

The current vocabulary of political struggle speaks of 'liberated zones'. In the associated propaganda war one man's liberated zone is often another's occupied territory. In Paul's world of sin and slavery and law the Christian community was the liberated zone. The unfree world is still with us. The witness and reality of the liberated zone of the Church is as necessary as ever. How real is it? How evident is it?

The Church has a thousand angles. It offers a thousand perspectives. Recognizing it as a 'liberated zone', community of the freed, involves angles and perspectives which differ for insider and outsider, associate and committed, cleric and lay, bishop and priest. For quite other but powerful reasons angle and perspective differ for rich and poor, for first, second and third worlds, for male and female. No one of these perspectives offers simple and complete truth. Yet one would hope — we are, as Paul might say, liberated in hope — that all angles and perspectives provide some evidence and experience of freedom. Do they?

THE EXPERIENCE OF FREEDOM

Feeling free may not be the ultimate test of liberated Christians. In the historical community of the Church laity ought normally and dominantly to feel free in relation to their priests, priests in relation to their bishops, theologians in regard to their clerical and episcopal Christian colleagues, women in regard to men. The 'feeling free' involves mutual respect, acceptance, trust. It involves a mutuality and equality which is not always evident, encouraged or even recognized. To recognize and encourage such mutual acceptance and trust it is necessary to provide the context, the continuous and frequently small-scale contact and community in which people can discover, express and develop their freedom. Paul's churches in Galatia and elsewhere provided this kind of context. Religious communities have institutionalized it, not always successfully. A rediscovery of it is recurring throughout the universal Church today in basic communities, particularly in the Third World and in a rich profusion of groups dedicated to prayer, peace and renewal. We need community support and structures to be free. That freedom involves participation in the work and decision-making of the community. Christian freedom as divine gift is mediated and expressed through Christian community. As mediated, freedom is caught, felt, assimilated in a community that knows itself to be free. As expressed, freedom develops the person and enriches the community. The creative works of Christian freedom renew the treasures of Christian community for new generations. In their liberated lives in the liberated zone of the Church, Christian laity and clergy offer to their contemporaries and successors the Spirit of freedom, whereby they were set free.

PERSONAL LIBERATION

For Christian freedom and its witness communal structures like laws and institutions are important and necessary, but not, as the scientists say, sufficient. Paul was well aware of this. Personal conversion is as necessary as structural conversion. In the actual case of the Galatians the two were inextricably

Set Free for Freedom

connected. To pretend to faith in Jesus while insisting on the old structures of the law for Gentiles involved self-contradiction. Paul was no less critical of personal self-indulgence on the pretext of freedom. The desires and works of 'the flesh' (unliberated man) are to be rejected and excluded from the Kingdom of God. These include 'idolatry and sorcery', 'fornication and impurity', 'enmity, strife, jealousy, and anger', 'drunkenness (and) carousing', and all forms of 'selfishness' (5:16-21). By contrast 'the fruit of the Spirit (of freedom) is love, joy, peace, patience, kindness, goodness, faithfulness, gentleness, self-control'.

These contrasting pictures of the licentious and liberated person draw attention to the personal structures of freedom and the personal conversion it involves. In another idiom the liberated person is the integrated person. Possibly diverging desires and powers come together in creative freedom. The licentious person remains unintegrated, with desires and powers fragmenting and conflicting. In the integrated but developing and dynamic, not static, person, the powers of creation fragmented by sin recover their direction and effectiveness. They become the powers of new creation. The liberated, free person acts out of these dynamic creative capacities which have been traditionally called virtues.

SETTING ONE ANOTHER FREE

Paul's insight into the liberated Christian as integrated and virtuous does not imply some kind of self-contained, isolated, self-sufficient being. The freedom and independence of the Christian is not the autonomy of isolation but the freedom of gift and of interdependence. The gift from God and dependence on him is crucial to Paul. No less essential is the relationship

The New Testament As Personal Reading

with neighbour. Here (Gal. 5:14) as in the letter to the Romans (13:9) Paul summarizes the whole Christian life as love of neighbour, taking the summary a stage beyond even Jesus. In loving the neighbour service to the point of bearing his burdens becomes the test of fulfilling the new 'law of Christ' (6:2). Here Paul is returning to the recognition, acceptance and mutuality implicit in his understanding of the Christian community and its freedom from divisions.

The freedom for community and person is now more intimately and explicitly connected with love and service of the neighbour. It is in that love and service that Christians express and receive their freedom. We are set free for and by one another.

The mystery of incarnation will always challenge us. That God was in Jesus reconciling and liberating the world and humankind will always remain for those who take it seriously barely credible and almost totally incomprehensible. We need signs and wonders nearer home. Neighbours provide these. Neighbours are these. They too may call God, Abba, Father by the gift of the Spirit. They also constitute the liberating presence of God to us. In love and service of neighbours we are summoned out of ourselves. By mediating the presence of God to us they enable us to go out of ourselves. Set free for them we become our true selves. The mystery of incarnation is focused in the mystery of neighbour. The mystery of Christian liberation takes flesh in our love for one another. Our highest dignity and deepest challenge as Christians is to set one another free by this power of God manifested and realized in Jesus the Christ.

Paul's charter of freedom embraces our whole selves and our whole world. It is personal, political and cosmic. It is liberation in hope and liberation in

Set Free for Freedom

history. The kingdom of the free is among us and still to come. In the community of the Church we dare to say: Our Father, who art among us, you have come to set us free. Our freedom, our commitment to the liberation of one another and of humankind is at once gift and call for us as it was for the Galatians. 'For freedom Christ has set us free; stand fast therefore and do not submit again to the yoke of slavery' (5:1).

The Passion According to Mark
— Divine Power and Suffering

John Riches

'For they were seized by terror and ecstasy and said nothing to anyone. For they were afraid.' Thus the culmination of Mark's passion narrative which, whether it be Mark's final word or no, brings us to the point where he would have us be: the women struck dumb in ecstasy at the first dawning of the resurrection light, silent, frail witnesses to that which Jesus' followers have consistently failed to see, to understand and to confess.

The way to those first dawnings of ecstasy is however a long and painful way, stretching from the first call of the disciples to their final betrayal, denial and flight. And this narrative which documents relentlessly their failure to understand, to receive Jesus' teaching or indeed his anticipated glory in the transfiguration extends on into and reaches its culmination in the remorseless exposure of Peter which is interwoven into the account of his Lord's trial and humiliation. Only at the end of this painful way of darkness and blindness, in which the full range of human weakness and infidelity is displayed, will the light shine out and snatch his followers up out of themselves into the unutterable beauty of his resurrection glory.

Talk of the unutterable beauty brings me to the other source of this meditation on the Passion. No one — or at least no Christian commentator — comes to the Passion narratives unburdened or uninformed.

John Riches is Lecturer in New Testament in the Faculty of Divinity at the University of Glasgow.

The Passion According to Mark

The personal history of each Christian's faith is marked one way or another by his encounters with the Lord of the Passion, be it in the devotions of Holy Week: of stations of the Cross, the Maundy watch, the preaching of the Passion or as one encounters him in the great works of Christian theology and spirituality of which for me two remain outstanding: von Balthasar's *Theologie der drei Tage* and, in a quite different mode, Studdert Kennedy's meditations from the Western front to be found in poems such as his 'High and Lifted Up' or more fully but less accessibly in his book *The Hardest Part*. Behind all this too lies for me the teaching and inspiration of Donald MacKinnon whose theological *oeuvre* has its centre in a search for illumination of the dark and desperate areas of human experience and who taught us to look for such illumination foremost in the figure of the one in agony in the garden who will indeed be in agony until the end of the world. All this to indicate the kind of questions for which I look to these chapters if not for answers, then pointers on the way.

And the question above all is a question about the nature of God and his *power*. The exultation of the *O felix culpa* is in a sense exchanged for the deeper questioning which probes beyond the Son's victory to ask what kind of God can allow his Son thus to suffer, can indeed create and permit to continue a world which holds such terrors for innocent and guilty alike? It was this quesion which Studdert Kennedy had to face when he first met the soldiers in the field hospitals of France and to them he offered in answer the figure of the crucified Christ. Yet *in itself* that figure is no answer: the officer to whom he refers in the preface to *The Hardest Part* throws it back at him:

The New Testament As Personal Reading

What do you mean? God cannot be like that. God is Almighty, Maker of heaven and earth, Monarch of the world, the King of Kings, the Lord of Lords, whose will sways all the world. That is a battered, wounded, bleeding figure, nailed to a cross and helpless, defeated by the world and broken in all but spirit. That is not God; it is part of God's plan: God's mysterious, repulsive, and apparently perfectly futile plan for saving the world from sin . . . I tell you that cross does not help me a bit; it makes things worse. I admire Jesus of Nazareth; I think he was splendid, as my friends at the front are splendid — splendid in their courage, patience and unbroken spirit. But I ask you not what Jesus *was* like, but what God *is* like, God who willed his death in agony upon the cross, and who apparently wills the wholesale slaughter in this war. Jesus Christ I know and admire, but what is God Almighty like? To me he is still the unknown God (*The Hardest Part*, pp. xiv-xv).

We cannot of course know for certain what precise form the questions which prompted Mark in the writing of his gospel took. Was he writing for the persecuted Church preoccupied with questions about God's apparent powerlessness, his unwillingness to intervene to save his faithful from Nero's tar barrels? Was he attempting to combat a view of Jesus' divinity, which saw him as akin to some 'divine-man' miracle worker of the ilk of Apollonius of Tyanna or to plead for a christology more firmly rooted in an understanding of the Cross? Was his purpose primarily apologetic: to argue to Romans that Jesus was not a revolutionary, political figure but that he had been crucified at the instigation of the Jews out of jealousy for his religious authority and power? Who can say

The Passion According to Mark

for sure? There is little doubt that Christians in Rome had undergone unimaginable horrors at Nero's hands and that the shock waves of the Jewish War will have reached Rome and its Christian community ten years later to reinforce the deep impact which such events must have made on Roman Christians. If we add to this the traditions which connect Peter's crucifixion with Rome and consider his central role in the gospel not to mention the traditions which specifically connect him with the authorship of the gospel, we have at least a basis in external evidence for the supposition that past persecution and the terrible fate of the Jews must have burnt themselves into the consciousness of Mark and his readers. Did not they too search for an answer to the question of human suffering? — of how God can allow his own people to undergo such horrors?

How then does Mark's Passion Narrative address itself to such problems, if indeed it does? Let me simplify. The narrative enfolds a double drama. There is first the drama between Jesus and men and women; his disciples, Judas, Peter, the chief priests, Pilate, the soldiers, the centurion, the women. And then hinted at, overheard rather than acted out openly, there is the drama between Jesus and his Father, his God. The first is, for want of better words, a conversion story; it is the story of Jesus' overcoming the enmity and betrayal of his friends and people, a story which admittedly allows us to see only the distant glimmerings of that conversion rather than portraying the full reversal of the human weakness and depravity which has been so fully displayed. The second is the story of an agony, of a terrible struggle between Jesus and his Father, God, a struggle for *understanding* won in obedience to an apparently implacable

The New Testament As Personal Reading

and terrible will, a struggle which nevertheless provides the basis for Jesus' struggle for the hearts and minds of men and women. Let us trace these through each in turn before we turn again to their resolution in the last verses of the gospel.

To describe Mark's Passion Narrative as a conversion story is at the least paradoxical, contrary to the appearances. In the most obvious sense it is the story of human depravity and weakness, of returning hatred, viciousness, cowardice for love, trust and confidence. Jesus, the one who has come to call men to follow him, to invite sinners to share his meals (2.17), to enter into fellowship with him, is betrayed by Judas 'one of the twelve', 'the one who eats with me'. The disciple and friend betrays Jesus to those who seek to seize him, is the agent by whom Jesus is delivered into the hands of sinful men for them to work their will with him. The very mode of betrayal chosen, the sign of fellowship and trust, mocks Jesus' very existence. Those who take the sword may perish by the sword, but Jesus perishes by the perversion and maltreating of the love and acceptance which is intended as his means of overcoming evil and enmity. Once seized Jesus is swept along by the tide of events; the forces of evil must have their way, as indeed was foreordained: the pretence of a trial, the false testimony, the buffetings, the handing over into the hands of the imperial power for condemnation, mockery and crucifixion. All the time it is his own who betray him, his disciples, the religious leaders of his people, his own people themselves crying out for his blood, mocking and jeering at him as he hangs on the cross. And not just mocking and jeering, but calling into question the reality and power of Jesus' mission: taunting him to save himself, to come down, to call on God to save

The Passion According to Mark

him.

And what of Jesus' other followers, those who do not actively work for his destruction? They are caught most cruelly in this unequal struggle between the powers of darkness and enmity and the weak, exposed figure of Jesus. Unable to measure the fierceness of the trial which lies ahead they are confused, distressed by his warnings and prophecies, questioning — 'is it I?' — blustering — 'Even if all lose faith, I will not'. As Jesus undergoes his agony in the garden even his closest followers fail him, absurdly inadequate, unable to watch, unable to pray. At the arrest their response is even more pitiful: a momentary flash of retaliation with its laughable fruits — 'the ear of the servant of the High Priest' — and then desertion and flight.

Leaving only Peter to taste the full bitterness of his powerlessness and weakness. Peter follows, albeit at a distance, right into the High Priest's palace, imagining to live up to his bold claim — even if all lose faith — but he is gradually driven off by a persistent, prattling girl, as his protestations and denials grow louder, echoing the false witnesses at Jesus' 'trial' in the courtyard within. His tears are tears of bitterness and despair, bitterness at his powerlessness and desperation in the face of defeat and the hopelessness of his condition.

Thus in one obvious sense this is a story of the bitterest reversal for Jesus' proclaimed Kingdom. The one who actively overcame demons, cured the sick, and announced God's only Kingdom of forgiveness and acceptance for sinners, now hangs in the place of the outcasts and criminals, condemned and rejected by the people he came to accept and to reconcile, rejected and abandoned by the Father whose love and forgiveness he has proclaimed and embodied. Even his followers, the Twelve who represent the twelve tribes of the new Israel, betray and desert and deny their 'king' as he is betrayed, falsely accused and condemned by his own subjects. The tiny beginnings of his Kingdom are swept away, the shepherd smitten, the little flock scattered. And yet Mark insists this is the way it was always intended, this was how it had to be, this is what was willed by God. This is the way God's Kingdom must be established and grounded. What kind of God? What kind of Kingdom?

Here we need to proceed with the greatest caution. Mark clearly deals with this question indirectly, hinting rather than giving his readers a full exposition. This perhaps not least because it is in the nature of the case that such things can hardly, if at all be uttered. But that he does deal with such questions is equally I think beyond doubt. What else is the nature of Jesus' struggle in the garden if not the struggle of the Son with his trust, belief, love in and for a Father who demands of him that he die? What kind of a Father is that? At least Isaac went unwittingly to his intended sacrifice. Here Jesus himself is to allow himself to be bound and carried off by wicked and evil men and there will be no ram in the thicket. And Mark furnishes us with enough clues in the temptation narrative and in the questions about power and authority among the disciples, indeed about the nature of the power of the Son of Man (chs. 8 and 9) to let us know the way his mind is running. God's power is not to be exercised or to be served by force, by great acts of power and coercion, nor by acts of dramatic rescue. The way that Jesus has to go is the way of the servant and the cross. To suppose that this is merely a temporary lapse or interlude on God's part, to sup-

The Passion According to Mark

pose that this is merely a temporary veiling or limitation of God's true power and authority, is to cast God as Satan, to confuse God's Kingdom with the kingdoms of this world. To reject the idea that the Son of Man must suffer is to play the role of the tempter himself.

Yet is not that what the Churches and the theologians have all too often done? Have they not seen God almighty as a God whose power is exercised through absolute authorship and relentless control of all things? And is not Studdert Kennedy's cry from the trenches:

> And I hate the God of Power on His hellish
>   heavenly throne,
> Looking down on rape and murder, hearing little
>   children moan.
> Though a million angels hail Thee King of Kings,
>   yet cannot I,
> There is nought can break the silence of my
>   sorrow save the cry,
> 'Thou who rul'st this world of sinners with Thy
>   heavy iron rod,
> Was there ever any sinner who has sinned the
>   sin of God?'

the true and proper rejection of all such distortions of God's power and will? No amount of sophistry, of talk about the permissive will of God or about evil as a deprivation of good should deceive us into denying that the horrors of war, of Nero's acts of wanton cruelty, of Auschwitz, of nuclear attack and the other countless abysses of human depravity are *contrary* to God's will and are positively *evil*.

But then what of the Cross? Does not God will, does not Jesus accept this suffering, this tortured death?

The New Testament As Personal Reading

That depends vitally on how we understand the object of that will and acceptance. If we conceive of the Cross as the punishment God inflicts on his creatures for their sins, borne now in their stead by his Son, then we make God the author of the torture and agony of the crucifixion and the priests, Pilate and the soldiers merely his unwitting agents. If we conceive of the Cross as the ultimate response of human depravity to God's offer of forgiveness and acceptance in Jesus' preaching and ministry, then God's willing of the cup and Jesus' acceptance of it are but the ultimate consequence of his will to love and forgive, viz. his readiness to go on bearing the suffering and rejection consequent upon such loving. And there can surely be no doubt where Mark stands on such an issue. The crucifixion is not the work of God but of wicked men who seize Jesus, who take him into their power and work their will on him. The whole drama from the betrayal to the mocking of the priests and the bystanders is as we have seen deliberately and painfully portrayed as a rejection of Jesus' saving message and work of love, acceptance and forgiveness, and the taunt is that God will not act to save him, to get him down from the cross. Nor will he.

Yet is God then powerless, does God abandon Jesus? Jesus in his prayer in the garden asserts precisely and paradoxically the omnipotence of God. 'Abba, Father, all things are possible for you'. How — and in what sense — is Jesus' acceptance of his cup, his allowing himself to be seized and borne off by his tormentors a remaining within the power and providence of God? Or to put it differently, what sense can be attached to the Fatherhood of God if it entails his abandonment of his Son?

Jesus' sayings in the garden and on the cross are

The Passion According to Mark

cast in the form of prayers — this by contrast with his earlier dialogue with Satan where he engages his adversary with scriptural texts. That is to say the question of the extent to which Jesus remains within the providence of God can be seen as a question about the continuance of his dialogue with the Father, for it is this which preserves him from temptation, which enables him to remain faithful. But is that dialogue sustained? Jesus' cry from the cross: *Eli, Eli, lama sabachthani*, seems to mark the breaking off of that dialogue on God's part. And indeed if God's care and providence is conceived of in terms of protecting from harm and misfortune, as well as of guiding, forgiving and restoring, not in itself an unreasonable interpretation of fatherhood, then Jesus' plight on the cross cannot appear as anything other than a falling out of his hands into the hands of wicked men. But that would be to reckon without chapter 16 and indeed without the repeated assertions in the gospel of the divine necessity of Jesus' passion and death. What then can we say? At the very least that such abandonment represents the final bearing of the consequences of God's loving will, the placing of itself into men's hands, the suffering and passion of *God* as he embraces that which is radically opposed to his own nature, without yet ceasing to be God. I think here particularly of von Balthasar's meditations, most conveniently to be found in English in his early work *The Heart of the World*. Loving 'to the end', says St John. It also, marks the end-point of Jesus' obedience, his obedience unto death on the cross, which obedience binds him to God, even beyond the active care and providence of the Father in the experience of his entering into the realm of sin and death. May we say more? May one suggest tentatively that Mark points here to a deepening of the Christian experience of God in prayer, to the point at which as the Son of God is obedient to his Father's unswerving will, he enters more deeply in the darkness of his abandonment into the mystery of God's will? If Mark insists as he does that the disciples will only learn understanding on the way of the cross, then does he not point to this place of darkness and abandonment as the true place of enlightenment and understanding? If Jesus is for Mark, despite the relative paucity of explicit instruction, still foremost the teacher, is it not here that illumination is to be gained, in the remaining true to the Father's loving will, in the discovery, in the bearing of its ultimate consequences, in the darkness of the vision of death, of the power which can bear all things and *overcome*?

But there's the rub! Wherein lies the overcoming? It can lie in nothing else than the power of love to attract, to draw men and women to it, to go on doing this despite all that they can do to it, despite death and destruction. I said that Mark's Passion narrative is a conversion story despite the appearances. Where all seems to be the reversal of what Jesus in obedience to his Father intends, there breaks in a light which takes the women by storm and strikes them dumb. They who, like the centurion, had stood watching him die, who had seen where he was buried, who had looked after his needs in Galilee, now come to pay their last respects, concerned with the practicalities, worrying about how they were going to get the stone rolled back when suddenly, wholly unexpectedly, they glimpse the dawning of a new world. The beauty of the resurrection, glimpsed only *via* the stone rolled back, the angelic figure in white, the empty tomb strikes them dumb with terror and *ekstasis*. The re-

The Passion According to Mark

versal of the reversal occurs in this vision of the awesomeness, beauty and glory of that love which rises triumphant because infinitely more real than all else. Suddenly the world which had seemed to triumph, which had seemed to dominate and subdue, to trample on this love is revealed in all its transitoriness and futility in the Easter light and the women are struck with terror as their worlds turn upside down.

In this one moment is revealed that which lies beyond all our notions of power and victory, the Kingship, the glory of God's love which is life itself and which overcomes by its sheer capacity to go on loving, to go on suffering, bearing, and forgiving and accepting all that this world can do. The resurrection is not a reversal of the crucifixion insofar as in his passion Jesus accepts God's will to go on suffering, bearing man's rejection of his love. It is precisely the reaffirmation of that will and the renewal of that agony: the light shines on in darkness and the darkness has not — and will not — overcome it. Christ will indeed be in agony until the end of the world, so Pascal; but while nothing must blunt our vision of the depth of that suffering love, we must equally not lose sight of the beauty and power of that living love which is broken and renewed and shared through the ages. The vision of the crucified, living Lord can speak to the officers of the trenches of the Western Front and their brothers and sisters in extremity everywhere, if only they can begin to see in that figure the one who embodies the true glory and power of God:

> For Thy glory is the glory of Love's loss,
> And Thou hast no other splendour but the
>   splendour of the Cross.
> For in Christ I see the martyrs and the beauty of
>   their pain

The New Testament As Personal Reading

And in Him I hear the promise that my dead shall rise again.
High and lifted up, I see Him on the eternal Calvary,
And two piercéd hands are stretching east and west o'er land and sea.
On my knees I fall and worship that great Cross that shines above,
For the very God of Heaven is not Power, but Power of Love.

Works referred to: H. V. von Balthasar, *Theologie det drei Tage*, Einsiedeln, 1969, also to be found as 'Mysterium Paschale', in *Mysterium Salutis III/2*, pp. 133-326, Einsiedeln, 1969. H. V. von Balthasar, *Heart of the World*, San Francisco, 1979 (available from T. & T. Clarke, Edinburgh). G. A. Studdert Kennedy, *The Hardest Part*, London, 1918. G. A. Studdert Kennedy, *The Unutterable Beauty*, London, 1943.

The Resurrection

Sister Josephine Newman

> Jesus as the Redeemer, brings us salvation in so far as he opens the way to 'resurrection', to a life entirely receptive to the divine light and Word, and therefore fit to be transformed into a new, supernatural mode of being (P. John, O.S.B., *The Divine Dimension*, p. 76).

As I read and reflect on the Gospel accounts of the Resurrection of Jesus Christ I find myself centering more and more on the inner journey through which life takes its form and finds its expression. For me this perspective more than any other illuminates the meaning and direction of my life as I strive to make my own the mystery of God's presence in the world. And so, as I share my reflections in these pages, I am conscious that I am neither scripture scholar nor theologian in any strict sense; that my understanding of scripture does not reflect the deep riches the modern exegete might portray. But I am conscious too that one's personal journey through life is the other perspective within which we live and that an understanding of the spiritual dimension of our lives can open to us the pathway of wisdom. Within each of us there is that place wherein wisdom is born and it is there the mystery of God's presence finds its deepest echo. This mystery, truly imprinted in the human heart, is encountered in and through the journey of

---

Sister Josephine Newman is a Dominican nun. She lectures in Moral and Political Philosophy at University College, Dublin.

one's self as it struggles to awaken and respond to the call of that presence within.

I

I want to begin, then, by taking up briefly certain aspects of our potential as spiritual beings and how we tend to relate to that potential in our present day culture.

It is conceivable that a person might go through life accepting unquestioningly the beliefs and doctrines of the religion he or she professes. But in our Western society this is no longer a common experience. As Enda McDonagh reminds us: 'So much conventional religious education and theological discussion has suddenly become meaningless because people could not relate it to their experience of being human' (*Gift and Call*, p. 4). We live in an age which is slowly emerging from the grip of positivistic thinking and the truth-searching mind still finds itself resistant and sceptical in relating to realities which have transcendent value and significance. Yet despite this and despite the temptation to bracket all questions about transcendence as meaningless there is ample evidence today of an intensified search at another level of human exploration, the level of self-consciousness. The dynamic of this search is most truly identified as the search for meaning. This search becomes the bridge between the person and the realities in which life is encountered. Put in another way it is the search of the self for an ever-widening life-context in which to ground itself in relation to its experience and from which to discover its own horizons more fully. More than anything else this search is a touch-stone of authenticity as the human person strives to realize the 'further reaches' of his or her innate human potential.

The Resurrection

Whether we choose to call it the search of 'self-surpassing consciousness' (Nietzsche) or 'self-transcending consciousness' (ethical-religious tradition) or maybe more aptly 'creative consciousness of self' (the phrase Rollo May suggests) it is a search that bears essentially on the spiritual nature of the human person. For to encounter life through the dynamic of inner meaning is to engage in a journey of self-discovery which leads us to be ever more open to our intuitive and receptive capacities. In this opening we experience both freedom from the barriers our personality-based self-consciousness creates and the inflow of self-transcending qualities in which life finds its truest expression.

But we might be tempted to query where the Christian stands in all of this. Isn't it true that the Christian already knows the answers to the meaning of life? That being so, it is surmised, the Christian's work is to live these answers, to put into practice the injunctions which are assured as pathways to eternal life.

Perhaps in this kind of thinking is betrayed one of the deepest misunderstandings of the search for meaning. Getting answers about life has little to do with the question of meaning. Its inner movement is not towards theoretical sophistication but towards sensitivity to deep experiences of one's own 'groundlessness' at any point of our development. The threat of this 'groundlessness' is experienced by everyone at some time or other. It is usually sensed as fear of nothingness or simply purposelessness. In reality, it is life's own inner thrust going beyond the boundaries we set ourselves so as to feel secure and grounded. In this way the self feels urged to centre and ground itself in ever-widening horizons and to transcend the established limits of conscious personality. When a person becomes part of this inner movement of life he/she does not *get answers about life*. Rather he/she begins to see things differently by taking a different stand and perspective on life. The self breaks free from the grip of its ever-present subjective fabrications and becomes, increasingly, part of a world of inner harmony with reality. This is the world of true being within which we come to experience the reality of unity, truth, goodness and the self-transcending qualities of life that spring from and give expression to these realities.

So the Christian, and in general the religious person, might easily overlook an essential key in understanding the religious dimension of life. Even more sadly, if the experiences of the searching self are blocked, the response of the human spirit to Christian truth may take form in a rigid, blind-faith acceptance of beliefs which close the human spirit to the very experience it tries to evoke.

II

When we come from within this perspective to consider the events in which the life and death of Jesus found expression we are indeed in the presence of the most significant and symbolic act in human life history. Here more than anywhere else we see the human spirit as it grapples with a mystery which transcends any boundary it might set itself. And as we read the gospel accounts of this mystic event, this exchange between the divine and the human, we can also see emerging in the consciousness of the followers of Jesus a search which led them to a radical shift in perspective in life the full implications of which could be realized only in the Pentecost reality. This exchange between the divine and human, this pene-

The Resurrection

tration of the human by the divine, changed the course of human life. For in stretching beyond itself to the infinite as the ultimate ground of its finite existence human life in the person of Christ opened to the gratuitous fulfilment of all its expectations (Rom. 8). The exchange is wholly gift, wholly grace, and for us it is an object of faith held in and through our life in Christ. Yet it illumines and directs our understanding of all human life as that life now encounters the steps of its own inner search for its ultimate meaning and ground.

As we look to the gospel accounts of the resurrection of Jesus we find portrayed there some of the difficulties the human person experiences in trying to grapple with this mystery. We might be tempted to think that the disciples of Jesus should have had little difficulty in understanding what it was all about. They had lived with him, walking with him and had listened and responded to his message. Yet, we know it was not so! Time and again we witness their puzzlement, perplexity and incomprehension. Plainly they did not at first understand the reality the resurrection expressed. There was the stone rolled back, the empty tomb, the linen cloths lying there. All of this symbolized a reality they were unable to envision. The sudden and dramatic revelation 'He is risen' was equally part of the scene of their puzzlement. So too with the subsequent appearances of Jesus: they did not recognize his changed mode of presence. Yet the familiar and significant word or gesture (John 20:15-16; Luke 24:30-31) opened their eyes to the reality of that presence. Clearly then their understanding was blocked and they recognized they were in the presence of mystery.

When we reflect more deeply on these scripture

The New Testament As Personal Reading

passages we find that the key to what was happening lay along a different path. He began to awaken them through the communications of his spirit. He 'breathed' on them the qualities within which the experience of his new mode of presence would become accessible to them. It was the kind of experience that would gradually change their lives in the context of his resurrection. Peace, above all, seems to be the quality he communicated, and forgiveness the key to peace. This peace he spoke of truly surpassed all understanding. It was the peace which links the person with his/her divine source, the ultimate reality. Peace, Jean Vanier writes, is 'a calling forth of my being . . . to be united and unite in the flames of the infinite . . .' (*Eruption to Hope*, p. 91). Love was the basic form through which his risen life was experienced. It was a love of deepest trust and encompassed even the reality of betrayal (John 21:15-18). Love, Jesus had told them before his passion, was the *new commandment* (John, Ch. 13). He gave them this commandment in the moment when he knew his betrayal was imminent. So too after his resurrection it was in the context of another form of betrayal that Jesus reiterated the centrality of his *new commandment* — to love in a manner that transcends all human limits. These and all the inner qualities of life which Jesus spoke of and instilled in his followers were to be channels in which his new mode of presence would be experienced. In opening to and receiving these life qualities from him in his resurrected life the disciples would come into relation with the divine source of their being on which their deepest reality depended. In the resurrected Christ they were to receive and be one with the Spirit of God. 'The spirit of the Lord has filled the whole earth' (Wisdom, 1:7).

The Resurrection

This, we are told is 'the fundamental insight in all religious experience' (Jordan, Op. cit: p. 115). This was the new context in which the lives of the disciples — and the lives of all human beings — were to take root. Through the Pentecost event human response would forever become an expression of the divine indwelling in man, that *immanence* which is 'the realization of transcendence in plurality' (Ibid.).

There is, of course, mystery at the heart of this reality of the Divine indwelling. And when we come in faith to reflect and meditate on the scriptures we come to receive insight and understanding as this mystery unfolds in and through our own personal experiences. But there is much to be said about our human response to it, about the pathway of self-transcendence to which it beckons us. The Christian whose life is centered on the truth of the resurrection of Christ is called to self-transcendence. But too often there is confusion about the nature of transcendence. It is not a call to transcend the human as such, but to transcend the limits of the human by opening those limits to the divine. As the inner journey towards self-realization unfolds the need to become aware of and to break through the psychological roots of the barriers and boundaries we set ourselves grows. As this happens we discover our inner freedom, the freedom at the centre of our being, which makes it possible for us to identify with ever deeper levels of our own reality. In this process we are, in fact, connecting more and more with our inner spiritual selves and with that thrust of inner life that moves us beyond the world of limit. It is in this that we come to realize the

---

A full development of this line of thought can be found in the writings of N. D. O'Donoghue e.g. *Heaven in Ordinarie* (Springfield, Ill.: Templegate Publishers, 1979).

full horizons of our existence. For ultimately life pushes itself even beyond its own limits as the finite opens to the infinite.

The experience of this ultimate horizon is the central aspect of mystery in human life. The mystic, the poet and the philosopher all point in its direction but its reality opens to us only from within the deepest levels of human experience. In the resurrected Christ we see this reality in its glory. But we know too that its gateway was the reality of his suffering and death. It is the same for us as we move towards the fullness of life. 'In our baptism we have been buried with him, died like him, that so, just as Christ was raised up by his Father's power from the dead, we too might live and move in a new kind of existence' (Rom. 6:4).

The death experience we speak of is in our lives each day; it is at the heart of life's journey. As we grow beyond our self-imposed restrictions on our inner growth we bring to birth a deeper, more creative, more real self within. But in doing just that we are 'losing' and 'dying to' the 'sensory' bound self within. In the 'dying to self', lived and appropriated fully, we begin to glimpse something of the dimensions of that inner death to which the mystery of the resurrection points. Traditionally the great mystics identify this as the 'negative dimension' and we can learn something of its reality from those who have tried to describe it for us:

> The 'I' that gradually appropriates its own nothingness is not itself nothing. Rather does it assert itself in the direction of total Reality, according as it comprehends its nothingness, for it is only in the light of full Reality that the basic dependence and relativity of the human condition manifests itself. . . . This is easily said, easily understood as

The Resurrection

a mere conception, but the appropriation of this concept is a slow and sometimes cruel process as we are forced to let go of the dearest and deepest part of our being. For deeper than all is the infinite into which we are called (O'Donoghue, *Heaven in Ordinarie*, p. 193-194).

The self-transcendence to which the resurrected Christ draws us is expressed most fully in this. Yet it must always be remembered that it is the finite itself that mediates this infinite dimension. The 'finite' is not destroyed, it is transformed. Transcendence, then, can never be thought of as 'over and beyond' the human. Rather, the mystery of Christ is the mystery of the human radiating the divine as its deepest centre. This truth touches the heart of the mystery:

Man as we know him is 'at home' in the finite; it is from the centre of this finitude that he opens himself to the infinite. But precisely because he is responsive to the infinite we can envisage a transformation of man, by which, while remaining finite, he would yet find his centre in the infinite pole of his being. This is what Christian theology terms 'elevation to the supernatural'. It can only be achieved latently and seminally as long as man lives within the terrestrial order, but it can conceivably find fulfilment after death (O'Donoghue, op. cit., p. 15).

The mystery of Christ's resurrection is the mystery of 'divine transcendence as incarnation, the inmost union of the divine and the human' (Jordan, op. cit., p. 87). It was truly beyond the disciples' vision until they could experience the inflow of the spirit of Jesus and give expression to their own lives in its context. In his life and death Christ had appropriated the full-

The New Testament As Personal Reading

ness of the negative dimension in human life. He affirmed the divine as the source of all life. In his resurrection he manifested the fullness of human response as it finds its inmost centre in the divine and radiates therein a 'new kind of existence' (Rom. 6:4).

III

It was St Augustine who reminded us that though man certainly could not be God he could well become conscious of his potential divinity because God is even more inwardly in man than man is in himself. And even as far back as the fifth century St Augustine could connect this idea with true self-awareness wherein a person experiences his/her 'innermost being'. The inner journey on which we have been reflecting in the context of Christ's resurrection is about this consciousness and potential development of the divine within us. We live in an age which is looking inward once again to discover the steps to life through the thread of inner meaning. Meaning, in this sense, is rooted in the desire to relate with our life's experience in a way that truly expresses what we are. For the Christian the full revelation of what we are is known in and through the person of Christ. We know that 'we live and move and have our being' in God. We know too that it is a question of what we may become, but that this knowledge can remain theoretical and ineffective in the development of our lives. What we may become can only happen in an authentic way if we connect fully with the thrust of life as it seeks to realize itself in and through our personal experiences. When we look and reflect on the resurrection of Christ from within this perspective we may find that our deepest need is to 'know ourselves', to know the features of our own lives and to know the way to our in-

The Resurrection

ner self in and through our personal characteristics. In growing in inner-self awareness we are moving towards that centre in which the infinite is our ground and in which the indwelling of the spirit of God can be realized. We are moving from a 'merely sensory "I" ' to 'the "I" of intimate realization of God's presence . . .' (Jordan, op. cit., p. 118).

The most vital questions for ourselves then must relate to the human context in which man's inner being can take root and find its direction. What are the limits we so continuously encounter? How do they arise? What, in our experience, is the larger context in which we stand when we prise open these limits?

We know from our modern psychological studies that the emergence of a conscious self in us moves through many phases of development. It is perhaps best characterized as a growing awareness of self as a centre in relation to the variety of experiences that constitute and span my life. In a most basic sense the self is constituted as a centre of free will and individuality. My personality develops around this centre and gradually gives me a sense of 'I' which is difficult to distinguish, but can be distinguished, from my personality. The context in which this development takes place is one of need-fulfilling interaction with my environment. My need to live, to be understood and accepted, to feel secure, to express myself, to risk myself to life — all of these and their related needs are at the source of my life's energy. Even more, both my positive life thrust — to love, unite and construct, and my negative life thrust — to hate, to separate and to destroy, find their most concrete expression here. Whether, in fact, I come to centre more around my positive or my negative life energies depends much on what happens in relation to my basic life-needs.

The New Testament As Personal Reading

If, however, I *do* come to a sense of myself in and through the events in this form of life-interaction I gradually begin to experience a certain freedom in relation to my personality and a certain responsibility for myself in caring for its needs. Perhaps it is at this point I begin to *experience* what it is to be a person in my own right, so to speak, and what is meant by personal freedom. Perhaps it is also at this point I begin to become aware of deeper needs within the self. Traditionally we associate the birth of this awareness with the practice of meditation and prayer. Today there is also a growing consciousness that these needs manifest themselves in and through an experience of crisis in relation to the meaning of one's life. But at whatever point and in whatever way the awareness comes, it is a call from deep within one's being to move towards the spiritual well-springs of life. Expressed externally it is a call to relate to one's life within a wider perspective, one that is more inclusive of all life, more in harmony with reality as a whole. This is a spiritual path of life and increasingly one's self moves in the direction of being a participant in life rather than a controller and manipulator of life. The transition depends on one's choice to break out of the limits of one's own life and its perspective and to open to the inflow of spiritual life energies. In doing this one disposes oneself to become a channel of love, peace, unity, compassion, creativity and other spiritual qualities. The choice is one of opening to receive the inflow of these qualities, for they spring from our deeper alignment with reality. It is not and cannot be a choice to bring about and control these qualities. We are, here, in the world of prayer and meditation, 'waiting on God' as Simone Weil might say. It is, nonetheless, a world which, for us, is fraught with its

The Resurrection

own hazards and illusions. In no way can we be exempt, then, from the wisdom of the ages in this respect. The transcendence of the self in this pathway of the Spirit is not a movement 'beyond' the personality and its needs. It is a changed way of relating to them which leaves space and gives direction to the inner spiritual self as it seeks to find expression in human experience.

As we move into this journey towards life and reality we take into ourselves the reality of the death we have spoken of. For in transforming my relationship to life from one possessing it for myself to creatively participating in its reality I encounter a real death. The death is to *self* as I strive to possess and manipulate life and to construct my vision of how reality ought to be. But I am drawn by my inner yearnings to go beyond this distortion and as I do so I learn to stand in the experience of deprivation which 'letting go' of my need to 'control' and 'hold' implies. The 'letting go' is a death but it evokes a deeper possibility of life within me because I relate to it from a centre of deeper unity and harmony. And so I journey on to the full horizons of my being. I can choose to ignore the call to move 'beyond myself' at any point. But the call is there if I choose to listen. To respond even to my fullest possibilities is to respond to the infinite, and this is where the inner search for meaning leads. This truth is made manifest in the risen Christ in whom the fullness of the Godhead came to dwell.

> Christ's gospel conveys the basic meaning of all life, as a 'birth' from God, who causes it and makes it grow in the trials of earthly existence which are a Passion, a Way of the Cross, yet a life leading towards resurrection by setting an aim higher than all other aims of men: a victory over

death (Jordan, op. cit., p. 110).

SUGGESTED FURTHER READING:

Assagioli, R.: *Psychosynthesis* (Northamptonshire: Turnstone Bks. Ltd. 1965).
Ferrucci, Piero: *What We May Be* (Northamptonshire: Turnstone Bks. Ltd. 1982).
Eastcott, M.: *The Silent Path* (London: Rider & Company 1969).
Haughton, R.: *The Passionate God* (London: Darton, Longman & Todd 1981).

Blood-dimmed Tide?
Thoughts on the Apocalypse

Thomas Finan

A book that provides no quotations, someone has said, is no book — it is a plaything. Well, the Apocalypse is no plaything. It is as full of quotations as *Hamlet*. I propose to get into it simply by giving out a few of them. The Apocalypse is no joke either. Most people know that much — the very word has acquired dire connotations. Yet we discover from those quotations that we have been speaking its strange prose all our life.

'I am the Alpha and the Omega . . .' (1:8). 'If anyone has ears to hear, let him listen to what the Spirit is saying to the Churches' (2:7 — and to every one of the Churches of Asia Minor). '. . . You are neither cold nor hot. I wish you were one or the other, but since you are neither, but only lukewarm, I will spit you out of my mouth' (3:15, f.). 'Behold, I stand at the door and knock . . .' (3:20). 'And day and night they never stopped singing:

Holy, Holy, Holy
is the Lord God, the Almighty' (4:8).

'They will never hunger or thirst again; neither the sun nor scorching wind will ever plague them ('Fear no more the heat o' the sun . . .') . . . and God will wipe away all tears from their eyes' (7:16, f.). 'And a great sign appeared in heaven: a woman adorned with the

---

Thomas Finan is a priest of the diocese of Killala. He is Professor of Ancient Classics at St Patrick's College, Maynooth.

The New Testament As Personal Reading

sun, standing on the moon and crowned with twelve stars . . .' (12:1). 'Babylon has fallen, Babylon the great has fallen . . .' (14:8). 'And there I saw a woman riding a scarlet beast . . .' (17:3). 'Then I saw a new heaven and a new earth . . . I saw the holy city, the new Jerusalem, coming down from God out of heaven . . .' (21:1, f.). 'I shall indeed be with you soon. Amen; come, Lord Jesus' (22:20).

And I have not mentioned the Four Horsemen . . . (6:2, ff.)!

These are *direct* quotations. One should also draw attention to the *implicit* way in which for centuries and millennia Christian liturgy and civilization has spoken 'apocalyptic' in face of the apocalyptic moments of death and judgement. In the great meditation of the *Dies Irae*. In the great Responsorium *Libera Me:*

> Free me, O Lord, from eternal death on the
>   fearful day
> when heaven and earth will be moved;
> Day of anger that day of ruin and misery, day
>   of grandeur and grief,
> When heaven and earth will be moved . . .

The same scene greets us in stone from the west doors of the great cathedrals. It is a vision of the 'last things' that stretches back to the Apocalypse, to Mt. 24 and to the 'Day of the Lord' in the Old Testament prophets. It is not a fashionable emphasis now. And we should indeed distinguish imagery from literal fact. But we should also distinguish fear from religious awe before the *mysterium tremendum*. The shudder of awe is mankind's highest faculty, somebody said.

Blood-dimmed Tide?

It would be nice to be able to go on from there and write on the Apocalypse under the conditions that hold for other books of the New Testament. That is to say, an already shared understanding, as of a classic play or piece of music of which we had to give not so much an explanation as a fresh 'interpretation'. But it is not easy to speak about a book as strange as the Apocalypse without some initial pedagoguery. And in any case we cannot pretend to the genius of a Pascal and expect our 'thoughts' to be anything more than 'pious' if they are detached from any over-all view of the shape and meaning of the book they are derived from.

But that is our very first problem. It can hardly be the Classicist only who is frustrated if he cannot see how the work he is reading hangs together as a unity. A unity, said the very Classical Aristotle, is what has a beginning, a middle and an end. Now in the Apocalypse we see a beginning and an end all right. We would be in really bad case if we could not, in a work of which the central theme is precisely 'the Alpha and the Omega, the First and the Last, the Beginning and the End' (22:13). The problem is to follow the steps by which we get from the one to the other. And no wonder. We consult the experts, and going no further than the Jerusalem Bible we find that the Apocalypse 'presents many difficulties: repetitions, interruptions in the sequence of visions . . . passages obviously divorced from their context . . .' We do some historical research and we find that this problem is as old as the book itself. For instance Dionysius, a third-century bishop of Alexandria, tells us that 'some of our predecessors rejected the book and pulled it entirely to pieces, criticizing it chapter by chapter and pronouncing it unintelligible and illogical, and the title false.'

But the obscurity of the book did not make the bishop reject it. He respected mystery, and would not condemn as valueless what could not be taken in at a glance. But what he further tells us about ancient criticisms of the *content* of the book can still be a mote to trouble the mind's eye. Especially the contemporary mind's eye, soft-focused as it is on *omnia vincit amor* (love overcomes everything). Christian love is indeed mentioned — 'you have less love now than you used to', the long-suffering Church at Ephesus is told (2:4). But what is this among so much that is written in the tone of 'Avenge, O Lord, thy slaughtered saints'? '. . . How much longer will you wait before you pass sentence and take vengeance for our death on the inhabitants of the earth?' (6:10). And the earth is harvested and its vintage trodden in the press of God's anger 'until the blood that came out of the wine-press was up to the horses' bridles as far away as sixteen hundred furlongs' (14:20).

Exegetes wonder whether the John who wrote like this can be the same John as the evangelist of love. A Manichean dualist would wonder more fundamentally whether such material can be inspired by the God of the New Testament at all. And in fact Dionysius records that some critics before him attributed the book to the dreamings of the founder of a way-out heretical sect.

Need we protect the flank of our own orthodoxy as we mention such questionings? We can do no less than go along with the bishop we have been quoting. After as fine a piece of stylistic analysis as you could ask for he concludes that the Apocalypse is not indeed by John the Evangelist, but is still from the pen of 'a holy and inspired writer'. The devil's advocate

Blood-dimmed Tide?

serves orthodoxy too. He highlights the initial difficulty, strangeness and obscurity of the Apocalypse. Such 'thoughts' as we arrive at will emerge from an attempt to make that strangeness more familiar and the obscurity a little more clear.

* * * *

The first obscurity we struck was in the order and sequence of the book. One suggested explanation for this is that in the properly apocalyptic part of the work, from chapter four on, two separate apocalypses have been run together. One way of reducing the result to some order for the understanding is to bear in mind that we are reading an 'apocalypse', to get a grip on some likely sequence of events in such a work, and then to allow for overlapping and consequent occasional disturbance of the sequence in the present 'contaminated' work. And that over-all 'apocalyptic' sequence turns on times of trial and the ending of trials. Trials past and to come and to be faithfully endured in chapters one to three. And in chapter six and following, trials of which the end is first *prepared* and then *accomplished,* prior to the definitive ending of *all* persecution and evil and the establishment of a messianic age. All this starting from and contemplated under an all-inclusive vision of the transcendent Father and of Christ in glory (chapters four and five).

Trials . . . and times of trial . . . (for Christian believers, of course). None of us but knows something of that from history ancient or modern. So we can postpone that subject for the moment and start from another thought. From that vision of the transcendent God and of the glorified Christ, receiving 'praise, honour, glory and power for ever and ever' (5:14).

The New Testament As Personal Reading

There is first the sheer fact of that vision. 'Apocalypse' *means* vision, revelation. The wilder connotations of 'apocalyptic' are secondary. 'This is the revelation', it begins, given by God through Jesus Christ. 'It was the Lord's day and the Spirit possessed me . . .' (1:10). 'I saw' he says again and again. What he sees in chapter four is the author of the universe, by whose will 'everything was made and exists' (4:11). And that vision generates the classical religious experience of the *holy*.

'Holy, Holy, Holy
is the Lord God, the Almighty' (4:8).

John borrows the words of the great vision of Isaiah (6:3). And here as in so much else he puts himself in the line of the great prophets and their moments of mystical vision. How often do we say or hear those words of Isaiah and John without realising that this is their original burden, the burden of the mystery, the *mysterium tremendum,* the transcendence before which we tremble with awe. And yet this experience is essential to vital religion. It is present not only in the grandeur of Isaiah but in the pastoral simplicity of the birth of Christ. 'The angel of the Lord appeared to them, and the *glory* of the Lord shone round about them, and they *feared* with a great fear' (Lk. 2:9). Without that vision moralistics and hermeneutics are empty cisterns, mills that grind without wheat.

Secondly there is the function of that vision within the book. The book, as we have said, turns on trials and times of trial — the common connotation of 'apocalyptic' is not unjustified. And in this respect we have to be fairly innocent of history not to see the Apocalypse as a permanently relevant book, however

Blood-dimmed Tide?

obscure the details of its meaning. I am indebted to a colleague for the remark of a friend of his, to the effect that he thought the Apocalypse 'a barbarous book' — until he witnessed the final bombarding of Berlin. If anything it is the kind of book without which we cannot come to terms with barbarism. And the deepest trial in such times of trial is the trial of faith and hope and meaning. The Apocalypse sets its times of trial within a vision of final order that looks to the goal of time, and a vision of transcendence that looks beyond time. It enlarges on Christ's own farewell words to his disciples. '. . . I have told you all this so that you may have peace in me. In the world you will have tribulation, but be brave, I have overcome the world' (Jn. 16:33). Sin is behovely, but all shall be well . . .

* * * *

The Apocalypse starts from this high demanding level. And the historical trials are evoked in terms that are visionary, imagistic and of course obscure. And yet among the fascinations of the book is the fact that we do glimpse concrete historical reality through it. It borrows the imagery of the prophets on the Day of the Lord and the persecutions of the chosen people. But it gives that imagery a local habitation. The book was written out of a historical persecution, or persecutions, of Christians. The persecutor, imperial Rome, is clearly identifiable behind the symbolism of 'Babylon the Great' and the 'Scarlet Woman' who rides the 'beast' with seven heads. '. . . The seven heads are the seven hills, and the woman is sitting on them' (17:9). There is the clear intention of pointing to a particular emperor or emperors — 'there is need for shrewdness here . . .' (13:18; cf. 17:10).

One such identification seems to be of the notorious

Nero (d.68). Thoughts on the Apocalypse cannot fail to include a famous passage in the Roman historian Tacitus. It describes Nero's persecution of the Christians as political scapegoats for a great fire that devastated the centre of Rome in 64 — a fire otherwise thought to have been deliberately started by Nero himself, to facilitate his grandiose building projects. The passage fleshes out the lived reality out of which the Apocalypse could be written. 'First Nero had self-acknowledged Christians arrested. Then, on their information, large numbers of others were condemned, not so much for incendiarism as for their anti-social tendencies as haters of humanity. Their deaths were made farcical. Dressed in wild animals' skins they were torn to pieces by dogs, or crucified, or made into torches to be ignited after dark as substitutes for daylight. Nero provided his gardens for the spectacle . . .' (Tacitus, *Annals,* 15.44, tr. Grant).

It is worth noting too that it is not out of sympathy for what he calls the 'notoriously depraved Christians' that this sulphurous critic of Nero gives his report. 'Their originator, Christ, had been executed in Tiberius' reign by the governor of Judea, Pontius Pilatus. But in spite of this temporary setback the deadly superstition had broken out afresh, not only in Judea (where the mischief had started) but even in Rome. All degraded and shameful practices collect and flourish in the capital' (ibid.).

Under the same Nero Sts Peter and Paul were to be put to death in the capital within a couple of years. They *could* be 'the two olive trees and the two lamps that stand before the Lord of the world'(11:4). If so, then the Apocalypse gives us a veiled contemporary glimpse of that momentous founding event. 'When they have completed their witnessing the beast that

Blood-dimmed Tide?

comes out of the Abyss is going to make war on them . . . and kill them. Their corpses will lie in the main street of the Great City . . . Men out of every people, race, language and nation will stare at their corpses, not letting them be buried; and the people of the world will be glad about it . . . because these two prophets have been a plague to the people of the world' (11:7-10).

* * * *

But the Apocalypse is more than a historical document about the past. Considered purely as literature it would have the permanent human value of a long tradition of great books written out of extreme situations which provoked meditation on ultimate questions, like the meaning of evil and of innocent suffering. But the Apocalypse is Scripture, with a claim to permanent meaning. And it is explicitly prophetic, having as its range the *whole* of history to its culmination. Under this latter aspect the book has an initial strangeness with which any thoughts about it must come to terms. A double strangeness, of content and form. Both are strange because they are truly 'apocalyptic' in the conventional connotation — prophetic of cataclysms that yet remain vague because presented through imagery and symbolism difficult to control, and in a time-frame without fixed perspective. An example is the 'four horsemen' of war, famine, plague and death.

A first solution is to observe that in this respect the Apocalypse is in no way different from, indeed belongs to, the same *genre* as, the eschatological discourse of Christ in Mt. 24, which telescopes into one vision the end of Jerusalem and the end of the world. A second solution is to look at actual history, as it has

The New Testament As Personal Reading

so often been, and more than ever in our own century. I mentioned Berlin earlier. But Berlin is only one localised instance of all that this century has experienced of collective suffering and death. Ours is the century which has learned to speak of mega-death, man-made. The Marne, Verdun, the Kulaks, the Jews, the Poles, Auschwitz, Dresden, Hiroshima, Prague, Budapest, Vietnam, Biafra, El Salvador, Lebanon, Northern Ireland. We have known them all. Not just one 'holocaust' but many. The total of man-made death for the century has been estimated at a round hundred million. One writer has suggested that to the traditional 'two cities' we should now add a third, the City of the Dead. 'I had not thought death had undone so many . . .' Son of Man, can these bones live . . .?

The initial strangeness of the apocalyptic form, or voice, can be overcome as easily as can that of its content. We do not even have to go back to the Old Testament *loci* on which John drew. We need only look at a certain kind of serious imaginative literature and art in any age. We might even be the better for so doing, if it helped us to decompartmentalize the sacred and the secular. Such literature and art often speaks with an apocalyptic voice. We need not go back to Virgil's 'Messianic' Eclogue. Our title is taken from Yeats's poem, *The Second Coming:*

> The blood-dimmed tide is loosed . . .
> . . . .
> And what rough beast, its hour come round at last,
> Slouches towards Bethlehem to be born?

He did not live long enough to find out. There is Picasso's *Guernica*. There is Goya's *Capriccios* and

Blood-dimmed Tide?

Disasters of War (no se puede saber por qué — we cannot know the reason why). Certain poetry before the first world war is full of apocalyptic forebodings.

> The last age shall be worst of all
>   And you and I shall see
> The sky wrapped in a guilty pall:
> Laughter on lips shall fail and fall, —
>   Anguish of not-to-be . . .   (Alexander Blok)

The historian provides us with endless *facts* about our historical experience. The apocalyptist may seem to obscure the facts, but for all that it is he who lets in some light. Because he looks for the meaning of the facts, he looks below the surface of events into their depths, and beyond the immediate happening to the eschatological. His visions and imagery may seem to put a blind between us and reality. But it is he who gives the deeper purchase on reality — by penetrating to the perception that only a mystery of iniquity is adequate to the enormity of the facts. A Great Beast is at the heart of the Apocalypse. 'I don't believe in the beast, of course,' says a character in William Golding's *Lord of the Flies.* 'As Piggy says, life's scientific, but we don't know, do we? Not certainly, I mean . . .'

But the Apocalypse does not stop with the mystery of iniquity. Precisely because its concern is with finality the end of its vision is an age when that mystery will be overcome. This is not the result of a point of view particular to John. It is the result of the centrality of Christ and the meaning of his accomplishment. As we have seen, the Apocalypse opens with a vision of Christ in glory. He has already redeemed men of every race and tongue. But this is only the beginning of the end-time that will see his reign established on

The New Testament As Personal Reading

earth. In this light the Apocalypse is like a great eschatological drama dealing with the end of the present age and the coming of a future world-era, and turning on a decisive struggle between God and Satan. In three acts: preparatory events ('beginning'), the struggle proper ('middle'), the *dénouement* ('end'). In this drama Christ is the 'hero' and the *dénouement* is the establishing of the Kingdom of God on a new earth with a new, heavenly Jerusalem as its capital. 'Then I heard a loud voice call from the throne, "You see this city? Here God lives among men. He will make his home among them; they shall be his people and he will be their God . . . The world of the past has gone . . ." ' (21:3-4).

This final vision may seem as strange in its own way as the cataclysms on the way to it. But we forget that Christ already spoke of the moment when 'all is made new and the Son of Man sits on his throne of glory' (Mt. 19:28). We forget too the vision at the heart of St Paul, the vision of the cosmos itself 'being freed like us from its slavery to decadence' (Rom. 8:21). The Apocalypse is the last book in the collected works which launch man's history in a 'paradise'. The Apocalypse closes the epic circle as epics do — in return and restoration.

If we cannot accept that closing of the circle in its literal terms it may be that we have sound philosophical, exegetical or theological reasons. But the reason should not be that we too have minds that are purely scientific and positivist. That we cannot visualise the material world as other than it presently is, however opaque, preposterous and pig-headed. That we are driven by no wonder about its final state and purpose. A historian who brought a philosophical mind to his researches has put the matter this way: 'Granted that

Blood-dimmed Tide?

civilizations are born and mature and perish, are we on earth merely to build — and then destroy — those civilizations that are but temporary structures, obsolescent machines, like a generation of termites building their galleried *termitaria* that will be destroyed and then reconstructed in the heedless permanence of the species?' It is the Judeo-Christian Scriptures that are most constantly and intensely concerned with an end-state that will not destroy but transform and preserve the world and all that man has lived in it. In that they are but the axis of the race. The race has never been able to do without this kind of vision, whether embodied in ancient myths of the Golden Age or in the various modern messianisms. Doubtless many are drunk. But not all. 'On the contrary, this is that which was spoken of by the prophet Joel: "And it shall come to pass in the last days (says the Lord), I will pour out my Spirit upon all flesh: and your sons and your daughters shall prophesy, and your young men shall see visions, and your old men shall dream dreams . . ." ' (Acts 2:16 f.; Joel 2:28).